# The House On McCully Street

MIRACLE STORIES THAT WILL ENLARGE YOUR VISION OF GOD

## By Gladys Blews Wilson

FOREWORDS BY NORMA BIXLER AND JOHN GUEST

Belleville, Ontario, Canada

THE HOUSE ON MCCULLY STREET:
Copyright © 2004, Gladys Blews Wilson

*All Rights Reserved. No part of this publication may be reproduced, stored in a retrieval system or transmitted in any form or by any means—electronic, mechanical, photocopy, recording or any other—except for brief quotations in printed reviews, without the prior permission of the author.*

All Scripture quotations, unless otherwise specified are taken from the *New American Standard Bible*, copyright © The Lockman Foundation 1960, 1962, 1963, 1968, 1971, 1972, 1973. All rights reserved.

Scriptures marked NIV are from *The Holy Bible, New International Version*. Copyright © 1973, 1978, 1984 International Bible Society. Used by permission of Zondervan Publishing House. All rights reserved.

Scriptures marked KJV are from *The Holy Bible, King James Version*. Copyright © 1977, 1984, Thomas Nelson Inc., Publishers.

In certain instances, last names have been omitted or changed to protect the privacy of the individual and their families.

**National Library of Canada Cataloguing in Publication**
Wilson, Gladys Blews, 1931-
    The house on McCully Street : miracle stories that will enlarge your vision of God / Gladys Blews Wilson.
ISBN 1-55306-711-8.--ISBN 1-55306-713-4 (LSI ed.)
Title.   1. Prayer groups--Christianity. 2. Prayer--Christianity. I.
BV287.W44 2004    248.3'2    C2004-900670-3

*Essence Publishing* is a Christian Book Publisher dedicated to furthering the work of Christ through the written word. For more information, contact:

20 Hanna Court, Belleville, Ontario, Canada K8P 5J2.
Phone: 1-800-238-6376 • Fax: (613) 962-3055.
E-mail: publishing@essencegroup.com
Internet: www.essencegroup.com

The Wednesday Prayer Group continues to meet every Wednesday morning 10:00 A.M. to noon at the Mt. Lebanon United Methodist Church, Washington Road, Mt. Lebanon, near Pittsburgh, Pennsylvania. The meeting is open to all those who seek a fellowship of prayer in the name of the Lord Jesus Christ.

If you attended the Wednesday Prayer Group in the past, we'd like to hear from you. Letters may be addressed to Gladys B. Wilson, P.O. Box 45, Darlington, PA 16115.

You may also write for information about the release date for a study guide for *The House on McCully Street*.

# Table of Contents

Acknowledgements . . . . . . . . . . . . . . . . . . . . . . . . . . vii
Foreword . . . . . . . . . . . . . . . . . . . . . . . . . . . . . . . . . . ix
—*Norma Bixler, Founder Cornerstone TeleVision*
Foreword . . . . . . . . . . . . . . . . . . . . . . . . . . . . . . . . . xiii
—*Dr. John Guest, Evangelist/Pastor Christ Church
    At Grove Farm*
Author's Introduction . . . . . . . . . . . . . . . . . . . . . . . . xix

## AN EXTRAORDINARY CALL OF GOD
  1. Witnessing a Miracle . . . . . . . . . . . . . . . . . . . . . 1
  2. A Message From God . . . . . . . . . . . . . . . . . . . . . 7
  3. Pot Roast and Hot Apple Pie . . . . . . . . . . . . . . 13
  4. Peggy, Can You Trust Me? . . . . . . . . . . . . . . . . 21
  5. The Blessing of the Gold Box . . . . . . . . . . . . . 27

## A REMARKABLE GIFT OF LOVE
  6. A Paralyzing Hatred . . . . . . . . . . . . . . . . . . . . 33
  7. Answers to Three Prayers . . . . . . . . . . . . . . . . 39
  8. Stand Up and Walk . . . . . . . . . . . . . . . . . . . . . 43
  9. A Wednesday Dose of Love . . . . . . . . . . . . . . . 49

## STRANGE THINGS BEGIN TO HAPPEN
  10. Saved by Grace . . . . . . . . . . . . . . . . . . . . . . . . 53
  11. All Things Work Together for Good . . . . . . . . . . 59

12. Never, Never, Give in . . . . . . . . . . . . . . . . . . . . . . . 67
13. Where's the Prayer Meeting? . . . . . . . . . . . . . . . . 73
14. Like a Mighty Wind . . . . . . . . . . . . . . . . . . . . . . 79
15. Trapped in the Dining Room . . . . . . . . . . . . . . . 85

## GOD CALLS A LEADERSHIP TEAM
16. The Blue Chair . . . . . . . . . . . . . . . . . . . . . . . . . . . 93
17. The Blind Receive Sight. . . . . . . . . . . . . . . . . . . . 97
18. Waiting for God's Will . . . . . . . . . . . . . . . . . . . 103
19. The Roots of Cornerstone TeleVision . . . . . . . . . 107
20. A Gift of New Songs. . . . . . . . . . . . . . . . . . . . . 115
21. Not Easy, But Victorious. . . . . . . . . . . . . . . . . . 121
22. A Healing Touch. . . . . . . . . . . . . . . . . . . . . . . . 127

## A NEW VISION FOR THE PRAYER GROUP
23. The Tea Party Was Over! . . . . . . . . . . . . . . . . . 133
24. Goodbye to McCully Street. . . . . . . . . . . . . . . . 139
25. Going Home with Jesus. . . . . . . . . . . . . . . . . . . 143
26. The Mystery of the Turned Chairs . . . . . . . . . . 149
27. God Calls a New Senior Pastor. . . . . . . . . . . . . 155

## OUR GOD CAN DO ANYTHING
28. A Praise and Worship Songbook. . . . . . . . . . . . 159
29. Looking Out for His Flock . . . . . . . . . . . . . . . . 165
30. Holding the Hand of Jesus . . . . . . . . . . . . . . . . 169
31. All Things Are Made New . . . . . . . . . . . . . . . . 173
32. We Are One in the Spirit. . . . . . . . . . . . . . . . . 181
33. Prayer Encompassing the Globe . . . . . . . . . . . . 189

# Acknowledgements
## and Appreciation

For Tibb Gethin's clear vision from the Lord that God wanted His work to be spread abroad through the pages of this book.

For my husband, Frank, who waited patiently with unshakable faith that the author would one day emerge from her desk with a completed book.

For my daughter, Robin, who converted the copy into an attractive format.

For my literary agent, Les Stobbe, who found the publisher of God's choice.

For my friends, Sally Fahringer and Bert Thomas, who continually reminded me of my commitment to write the prayer group stories.

For the help of Carol Nomides, the current leader of the prayer group, and her husband, Charles, whose video tapes assured accuracy.

For Ernie Frederick, whose footsteps our family has tried to follow in his pioneering style of prayer walking.

For Carole Sanderson Streeter, editor of some transcripts.

And above all, for the members of the Wednesday Prayer Group who have contributed their stories and who continue to pray for the readers of this book.

# Foreword
## *Norma Bixler*

The day Tibb Gethin led me to say "Yes," to Jesus, we knelt in prayer and felt the Spirit of the Lord surrounding us. God's presence was so real that Tibb said, "Norma, this must be for something special."

Within a short time, I received a vision from the Lord. It showed me God's plan for my husband Russell and me to establish a Christian television channel in Pittsburgh. How could a young pastor and his wife with no money and no television experience accomplish such an overwhelming task?

Tibb was there to encourage us and pray for us. She and the Wednesday Prayer Group prayed us through the ten-year struggle to get the Lord's signal on the air. The group continues to pray for us today as we move forward into a third decade of ministry through Cornerstone TeleVision.

Over a twenty-three-year period, we have received 1.3 million counseling calls. Nearly 20,000 people have let us know that our programming led them to commit their lives to Christ. What began in Pittsburgh now reaches people by satellite across the United States and Canada and as far south as Central America.

In 1989, God spoke to Tibb and told her to gather together some of the stories of His work through the prayer group. She told me that God wanted her to extend the miracle of His saving grace and power beyond the limits of the prayer group into a world her heart ached to reach.

The stories she gathered are in this book. They are the witnesses that God worked unique miracles of physical healing in her home and in the church where the group moved when it outgrew her house. They are the stories of lives transformed, as mine was, when people committed their lives to our Lord Jesus Christ.

In this book, you will read about a few of the endless possibilities of life in the family of God. You will read about one woman's unquestioning obedience to the God she trusted and loved. I can still hear her saying at the beginning of every meeting: "What will God do today?" Her excitement was contagious. And God never let her down.

"God can do anything, Norma. He's Majestic, Powerful, Dynamic," Tibb said to me.

I never knew these things before she taught me. And she taught me to pray. She set an example of love and purity, which form the gateway to an effective prayer life.

Russell and I went to see Tibb when she was in Allegheny General Hospital before she died, and she said, "Don't pray for me to be healed. It's my time to go home to the Father." I wasn't ready for her to go. She was my spiritual mother, and we're never ready to lose our loved ones.

We thank God that He blesses us with our memories and Tibb has blessed us with a book that extends the memory of His work through her to future generations.

## Foreword

Tibb had faith that God would use the book, as He uses the prayer group, to let people know that God has a glorious plan for their lives.

It is my prayer that you, too, will catch Tibb's vision of the Almighty and her joy in approaching each new day as an adventure pre-planned by the Holy Spirit. What "something special" does God have in mind for you? You'll never know until you take that first step of faith, as I did in Tibb's living room on McCully Street.

*—Norma Bixler, Founder*
*Cornerstone TeleVision Network*

# Foreword

## Dr. John Guest

The great struggle in our lives is, who is going to run them? Who's going to be King? It's a lesser question to ask "Is this right, or is this wrong?" The heart of the spiritual conflict is, "Who is going to run the show?" The truth of the matter is that we want to run our own show, and when God breaks into our lives with the power of the Holy Spirit, He is putting that question to our hearts and minds.

This was the question I faced in 1954 in Harringay Arena, London, when confronted by the claims of Christ through a message by Billy Graham. Who was going to run my life? I believed I was a sinner. I knew Christ had died for my sins. I wanted His love in my life. I wanted His forgiveness. I wanted to go to heaven and not hell. But I did not want to surrender my autonomy! That was the battle that raged in me that spring evening in London.

I knew that day that I could not "come to Jesus" unless I gave Him the right to do whatever He pleased with my life, and although my mind could not comprehend it that day, within my spirit I knew that this commitment to the

Lord Jesus Christ would give me a sense of destiny. When I capitulated to Him, a flood of joy overwhelmed me. When push came to shove, God's grace became irresistible.

Within a year of that night I walked down the aisle in a London stadium, Tibb Gethin stood transformed by the same power of God in the aisle of a Pittsburgh auditorium. She writes that she felt her spirit bow before the Lord in the presence of His Holiness. She was convicted of her unworthiness and sin. Prior to her surrender, anyone who knew Tibb would say she was a good woman, a good wife and a good mother. She was a nurse who was making her mark as a teacher of pediatric nursing. She was a nurse who made waves by insisting that nurses of all races in hospitals where she served must be treated with equality. She was active in her church. She had made a childhood confession of faith in the Lord Jesus Christ.

The question she faced that day in Pittsburgh was one of submission. Does God have the right to ask that you make your life a living sacrifice, as the Apostle Paul teaches in his letter to the Romans? She was standing in the aisle at a Kathryn Kuhlman service. She didn't like the flamboyant style of the evangelist. She didn't believe that God was active today in the same way He was more than 2,000 years ago. Yet she was watching as the Lord God poured new life into her sister-in-law, Dolly Graham, and healed her of a terminal heart condition. With her own eyes, she saw God perform a miracle of healing, but that was not what transformed Tibb Gethin's life. What transformed her life was her answer to the eternally significant question, "Will you serve Me with heart and mind and soul and body?" And that's what she committed herself to do that day by the power of the Holy Spirit.

*Foreword*

Gladys Wilson's research presents the evidence of the commitment Tibb made that day. There are stories here about people who came to Tibb's Wednesday Prayer Group where God touched their lives and called them to go out and change the corner of the world God assigned to them. For some, this meant taking the power of the Holy Spirit into their homes—and that may have been a more difficult assignment than some others received, those who yielded their lives to an overseas missionary call, or a call to revitalize a church or a city or a territory marked out by a television channel dedicated to proclaiming the glory of God, or the task of starting a prayer group in another city, state, or country. Through the lives of the people recorded in this book, you will get a glimpse of what God intends our lives to be.

The late and legendary African bishop, Festo Kivengere from Uganda, who was ordained in St. Stephen's Episcopal Church where I was later to serve as rector, was a relatively new Christian when God led him to spend time at Tibb's prayer group. His life became intertwined with some of the people in this book. Ernie Frederick's faith was nurtured through the group, as they prayed for him and supported his work with troubled children in Pittsburgh, until God called him to his current missionary work that straddles two continents.

How many prayer groups did the Lord spin off after the model of that Wednesday Prayer Group? God alone knows the answer to that question, but I can tell you about one such meeting where my life converged with Gladys Wilson, the author of this book, and with Tibb.

It was a prayer and praise service on Sunday evenings at the Mount Lebanon United Presbyterian Church. This was Gladys Wilson's church, and we had met when Decision

## The House on McCully Street

Magazine sent her to write the story of my conversion and college ministry. The elders in her church gave Gladys permission to start a Sunday night prayer-and-praise meeting modeled after Tibb's group. Gladys asked me to be the speaker at the first meeting, and that night I met Tibb Gethin for the first time. Each week for ten weeks, a different speaker came to the meeting that Dr. David Barnhouse moderated. David was the son of the famous preacher Donald Gray Barnhouse. Many stories could be told about those meetings. But the amazing sequence of Bible studies brought by each speaker was a patent demonstration of the Holy Spirit's leading—beginning with me. I spoke that first night on Isaiah 61:1. Some 150 people attended the meeting. Gladys reminds me of how the folks who gathered enjoyed my English accent and pronunciation of Isaiah. But the message of the prophet Isaiah:

> *The Spirit of the Lord God is upon me, Because the Lord has anointed me to bring good news to the afflicted; He has sent me to bind up the brokenhearted, To proclaim liberty to captives, And freedom to prisoners,*

became the theme of every teacher's presentation. Every week, ten weeks in a row, every speaker who came to the Sunday night meeting taught from that same passage of scripture, unsolicited. Gladys, David Barnhouse and the leadership of that group stood in awe of the power of God to direct His messengers in such a prophetic fashion.

My prayer is that as you read this book you will stand in the presence of the Lord Jesus, as I did in a Billy Graham Crusade and as Tibb did in a Kathryn Kuhlman Healing Service in Pittsburgh.

## Foreword

The life of Tibb Gethin and those around her will make it clear how you can become intimate with the Lord Jesus Christ. It will also give you a window through which you will see Jesus at work in the lives of people and in the affairs of this world and see yourself included. It will encourage you to believe afresh what the Bible has to say about the Lord Jesus and how you, too, can experience the work of the Holy Spirit in your life.

—*Dr. John Guest, Pastor*
*Christ Church at Grove Farm*

# Author's Introduction

## *The House on McCully Street*

> *"And I will put My Spirit within you and cause you to walk in My statutes, and you will be careful to observe My ordinances"* (Ezekiel 36:27).

THE JULY MORNING WHEN I MET TIBB GETHIN, the temperature hovered between eighty and ninety degrees and the oppressive humidity level charged the air with a moist, vibrating heat.

My friend, Sally Fahringer, led the way up the steps onto the small porch of a Mount Lebanon duplex. It was 9:30, and Tibb stood by her front door hugging those who were flocking to the ten o'clock Wednesday morning prayer group. "We've been expecting you, Gladys," she said as she wrapped her arms around me and crushed me against her crisp pink-lace dress.

She reminded me of England's Queen Mother, and I soon learned that Tibb's elegant manner of dress was significant. She believed that she was leading others into the presence of the God of the Universe—the one who is King of kings and Lord of lords. When people came to seek her help, she was quick to tell them that she could do nothing for them but she knew the One who could. "I'll introduce you to Jesus, and He can do everything."

Released from her ample bosom, I stepped into a small living room filled with folding chairs and looked through a wide archway into a dining room where the table was pushed back to accommodate more chairs. The rooms were already filling with people, and Sally recommended that we sit on the stairs, which had a good view of the place where Tibb would stand to lead the regular weekly meeting of the Wednesday Prayer Group.

"I always come early so that I can sit on the stairs," Sally said. "By ten o'clock, this room will be jammed and people will be standing outside at the windows."

It was 1965, and Sally couldn't hide her excitement that, after years of invitations, she had finally persuaded me to attend the prayer group. While others gathered, she told me some of the group's history, and later I learned more from Tibb and from Kathryn Kuhlman's book, *I Believe in Miracles*.

The Kuhlman book, published in 1962, includes among other "miracle stories" the way in which God led Tibb to take her sister-in-law, Dolly Graham, to Kuhlman's miracle service in Pittsburgh. Consulting doctors agreed that Dolly's heart condition was medically incurable and she had only a few months to live.

"You have to understand the circumstances under which Dolly was miraculously healed before you can understand the development of the Wednesday Prayer Group," Tibb said to me when we met in her home in October 1994 to talk about the book "God told her to write."

Tibb was eighty-six years old in 1994, and said she had

## Author's Introduction

clear direction from God that she should implement the writing of a book. In preparation for this writing, she had met with other leaders of the group and people who had attended the prayer meeting for many years. They had prepared three videotapes in which individuals told the stories of their changed lives and miraculous healings. Several friends within the group suggested that she meet with me to talk about writing the book for her.

My name was suggested to her because of my experience as a newspaper writer. Tibb wanted the book to be written in a journalistic style, bringing the facts to life as the people living the story perceived them. In addition, I remembered some of the early meetings in her home and the transition from her home to the Mount Lebanon United Methodist Church. As an inveterate record keeper, I had kept notes related to the group until I moved from Mount Lebanon to Beaver Falls, Pennsylvania, in 1977. As a reporter, I haven't editorialized on the content. I simply put the stories into easy to read prose.

Tibb was as clear in her description of what God wanted the book to be as she was about her direction from God in 1955 that she should start a prayer group in her home. Her final word to me was the imperative that nothing in the book should glorify her.

"God alone must be glorified for all His mighty deeds," she said. "This book must have one purpose only—to glorify the name of Jesus and win others to serve Him."

Once she had made this abundantly clear, she began to tell me how God founded the prayer group.

# Chapter 1
## Witnessing a Miracle

*"For I, the Lord, am your healer"*
(Exodus 15:26b).

TIBB GETHIN DIDN'T COMPLAIN WHEN HER HUSband, Wynn, announced that his company was transferring him from St. Louis, Missouri, to Pittsburgh, Pennsylvania. With the experience of fourteen moves in twenty years, she considered herself an expert on relocating. Their only son, Dick, was completing his freshman year in college, and for the first time in many years, the Gethins would be living only a short drive from Indiana, Pennsylvania, where they had grown up and where many relatives continued to make their homes.

She was happy that Dick would be able to see more of the grandparents he had enjoyed visiting as a child. Her own plans included spending as much time as possible with Wynn's sister, Dolly Graham, for doctors had told Dolly that she had only a few months to live.

"I dearly loved Dolly," Tibb said. "She and I hit it off from the first time we met, when Wynn took me home to

## The House on McCully Street

meet his family on a college holiday. We kept in touch by phone and mail and saw each other when the family got together. I knew Dolly had heart trouble, but from a distance, it was possible for me to deny the severity of her illness."

The first time Tibb and Dolly got together in Pittsburgh, Tibb was shocked at the way Dolly's heart condition had changed her.

"She had been a dynamo of energy, and now she was in such a weakened condition that the slightest exertion left her breathless. Even eating was a strenuous exercise for her weak heart. She slept on four pillows—practically sitting up in bed—and frequently woke up during the night barely able to breathe," Tibb said.

"As a nurse, I knew only too well what a pulse rate of 126 beats a minute meant. She was taking digitalis to slow it down. She depended on her husband to help with the simplest household chores, and he had to carry her up the stairs at night and down in the morning."

Wynn's mother lived in Pittsburgh, too, and she told Tibb she had taken Dolly to a Kathryn Kuhlman healing service. Many people claimed to be healed at these weekly meetings at the old Carnegie Free Library on Pittsburgh's north side. Tibb knew how discouraged Dolly was, and she believed that when everything else failed, some people turn to prayer and the possibility of divine intervention.

Tibb, however, was not one of those people. She told her mother-in-law that she had no use for faith healers and didn't approve of giving people false hope when they were dying. She felt she could help Dolly in various practical ways, and she hoped medical science would find a way to repair her damaged heart.

Tibb paused in the telling of her story to pour a glass

of orange juice. She was not a tall woman, but she had stature. Although her voice was gentle, she spoke with such confidence that what she said commanded attention. For all of that, her inner humility was reflected in a smile that began slowly, broke over her face like sunshine and often ended in infectious laughter. Her piercing brown eyes might have been intimidating if not for the laughter lines etched in their corners.

Two months after the Gethins settled into their new home, Dolly phoned to ask Tibb if she would accompany her to a Kathryn Kuhlman meeting. It was a scorching hot July day and Tibb was trying to get her ironing done before noon. The duplex the couple had bought in Mount Lebanon wasn't air-conditioned, and there was no such thing as wash-and-wear shirts at that time. Years later, Tibb remembered the heat, her desire to finish the ironing and her lack of enthusiasm for Dolly's suggestion.

Dolly sensed Tibb's reluctance to go with her and so she tried to describe the excitement of attending a worship service where people were instantly healed through prayer. She told Tibb the service was less formal than the ones in the Methodist church. There was no printed program, and the evangelist said that she allowed the Holy Spirit to direct the meetings.

Dolly was trying to be persuasive, but every word she said was convincing Tibb that it wasn't a meeting she wanted to attend. Tibb said she'd call back shortly with an answer. She really wanted time to think of a credible reason why she could say "No" without telling Dolly she didn't believe in supernatural healing. She wanted to remind Dolly that Wynn's mother had already taken Dolly to a Kathryn Kuhlman service and she hadn't been healed.

"I'm often direct to a fault with people, but I knew I couldn't shatter Dolly's hope or question her 'revelation of God' during the Kuhlman meeting," Tibb said. "Dolly told me that while she was in the service watching as a young mute girl was instantly healed, she saw a dazzling brightness coming through the ceiling of the auditorium where the service was held. The light was so brilliant that she had to cover her eyes to shield them and she began to cry.

"No one else saw the light and they didn't know why Dolly was crying. At the same time, Dolly felt as though something had taken hold of her and she felt squeezed all over. From that day on she had an intense desire to study the Bible, and for the first time in many years she started to attend a church."

When Dolly told Tibb about "the revelation," Tibb acted as if she accepted it, but actually she thought her sister-in-law might have been hallucinating. What else could Tibb think when Dolly was so weak she couldn't hold a hymnbook? Someone else had to hold it for her, and she couldn't sing more than a few words without gasping for breath. However, she was experiencing a strange kind of euphoria. It didn't seem to matter to her that she wasn't physically healed. She talked about having peace and quoted a Bible verse about a peace that passes understanding.

Dolly wasn't preachy about her experience; she was imploring. It was as if she was saying, "I've got to go back there, and I'll have to go whether you go or not."

Tibb felt compelled by her love for her sister-in-law to say "Yes," whether she wanted to go or not. She called Dolly back and Dolly told her what time her husband would pick Tibb up, for neither of the women were licensed drivers.

Twenty minutes from Tibb's home on McCully Street,

they crossed the bridge from downtown Pittsburgh into the north side. Even before they got to the building where the miracle services were held, they were caught up in traffic and when Dolly's husband dropped them off, they found themselves in a sea of people waiting to get into the auditorium.

"I have no idea how we got inside the door. A way seemed to open, and unbelievably, we could see two empty seats way up front. With the help of an usher, we squeezed through the crowd to get to the seats," Tibb recalled.

By the time they were settled, Tibb felt uncomfortable and wished she hadn't agreed to come. Dolly's enthusiasm, however, was contagious, and Tibb joined her in thanking God that they had made it through the crowd.

In the very beginning of the service, Kathryn Kuhlman was praying for a woman with multiple sclerosis. In the midst of the prayer, she looked up and called out that someone was receiving a heart healing. Tibb glanced over and saw that Dolly's color was changing from a cyanotic gray to a healthy pink.

"I was seeing a transformation in Dolly, and it looked like some kind of power was going through her. I watched first with the curiosity of a nurse observing medical symptoms. Then, I watched with awe as Dolly was transformed," Tibb said.

"Her fingernails instantly turned from blue to pink. Color suffused her face as though she were receiving a blood transfusion. I knew instantly that I had never until now had a true vision of God's power. The same power was surging through me, as I now know, transforming my mind and my spirit."

She felt her spirit bow before the Lord. In the presence of His holiness, she was convicted of her unworthiness and sin.

How dare she doubt that God could do whatever He chose to do in the same way He had acted in the lives of men and women in the past? What had she been thinking to come here without expectation, as if she were doing God a favor to honor Him with a trivial kindness to her sister-in-law?

She knew in that instant that her "heart condition" was as terminal as Dolly's and that God had rescued her from the mediocrity and skepticism of a lukewarm faith. Then she heard an inner voice saying, "You are here so that you can go and tell this story."

Her mind received this message without question, and no thought of how the telling of this story might affect her life intruded itself into the glory of that moment. Tibb yielded to the power of God, and she felt a sense of tangible love crowding out every self-centered thought and desire.

Anyone who knew Dolly could see the extraordinary way in which God had healed her. Tibb's transformation was hidden like a seed planted in good ground that would grow and produce fruit beyond anything she could imagine at that moment. Within a few weeks, God called Tibb Gethin into a prayer ministry that spanned forty years.

The Wednesday Prayer Group that began in her home after Dolly was supernaturally healed continues to meet in the Mount Lebanon United Methodist Church. It is a place where people find healing of body, mind and spirit. God alone knows how many thousands of people have come to know Jesus Christ as their personal Savior through this group and how far reaching their witness is. The remarkable stories of God at work through Tibb's yielded life fill the rest of the pages in this book.

# Chapter 2
## A Message From God

*He said, "Go and tell this people..."* (Isaiah 6:9).

TIBB DIDN'T TAKE ANY CREDIT FOR STARTING THE prayer group in her home that grew so large she had to move it to her church. She was a nurse whose natural gifts had led to teaching pediatric nursing. Wherever she lived, she also taught Sunday school classes and was often asked to speak at women's meetings and conferences. She interpreted God's inner direction to tell others about His power to heal as a direction to tell other people through these established teaching assignments. Her most immediate concern was the women's Sunday school class she taught at the Mount Lebanon Methodist Church. She told them of her experience at the Kathryn Kuhlman meeting and began to weave her new knowledge of God's power into her lessons. She was met with skepticism that mirrored her own attitude when she felt obligated to take her sister-in-law to the Kuhlman

Miracle Service. On the one hand, she understood the negative feedback she was getting from the women, but on the other hand, she expected God would work miracles in the lives of these women, too.

In the meantime, Tibb and Dolly had a mutual passion for Bible study and a new openness to accept the truth from its pages. Each studied the Bible daily at home, and one day each week, Dolly's husband John drove her across town from Trafford to Mount Lebanon so that the two women could share their study and prayer.

They sat at the kitchen table, opened their Bibles and began to read from the Gospels to learn more about the ministry of Jesus. They prayed, and their prayers were exultant with praise for the miracle He had granted in their lives. They asked for nothing more than to sit in His presence and glorify this One whose love had become real to them. Each week, they were overwhelmed with the same sense of adoration and praise they had experienced on the day Dolly was healed.

"Prior to this time, I had heard the Bible stories about the healing ministry of Jesus and His disciples," Tibb said. "But, as far as I was concerned, these things had no relevance outside the pages of the Bible. They didn't happen today. God was out there somewhere, but He didn't really involve himself in the specific details of our lives. Prayer was an important ritual that made some kind of generalized connection with the Almighty.

"The death and resurrection of Jesus seemed unreal to me in the sense that it was distant. Now, through the pages of the Bible, I was learning and internalizing the fact that Jesus, who is truly God, actually loved me enough to suffer and die because of my sin."

Her experience of a childhood conversion was similar to that of many of her contemporaries whose parents were Christians and took them to church every Sunday.

"When I was nine years old, which was during World War I, I was emotionally touched by the Easter story. I tried to understand what 'sin' was," Tibb continued. "I knew that I was sometimes rude to my parents. I cheated occasionally in school or took things out of the stock in my father's grocery store without telling him. I knew these were sins, and I went forward in that little country church to confess these childish sins and receive absolution. But nothing changed, because I didn't know until the day Dolly was healed and I was spiritually transformed that Jesus had given me the power of the Holy Spirit to direct my life."

Her training as a nurse taught her to believe in science, not religion, as the remedy for human ills. As an adult, she hadn't abandoned her faith, but she had pushed it into the background as she devoted her life to intellectual rather than spiritual matters. "I had a passion for knowledge and pursued it with all my heart," she said.

Her son, Dick, remembers her excellent mind. "My mother was an avid reader, and when I was about ten years old, she took a college calculus course. I have no idea why mastering calculus was important to her, for most of the other students were graduate engineers. My dad, who was a ceramic engineer, helped her, and I was amazed when she asked me to help her master the principles too," Dick says. "While she was drawing me into this world of learning, she'd say, 'I'm never going to make this,' but then she came out with one of the top grades in the class."

After high-school graduation, Tibb enrolled at the Indiana Normal School (now Indiana University of

Pennsylvania), followed by further training at the University of Pennsylvania in Philadelphia and the University of Alabama at Tuscaloosa. She graduated from Western Pennsylvania School of Nursing and continued her education with post-graduate work in pediatric nursing at Bellevue Hospital in New York. Her training in the medical profession made her skeptical of claims that God continued to perform healing miracles.

One night two months after Dolly was healed, while Tibb stood at the kitchen sink washing dishes, the Lord spoke to her again. "Now is the time to start a prayer group," the Lord said to Tibb. "He didn't speak to me audibly, but He spoke just as clearly in my spirit," she said.

She didn't question that it was God speaking, and she was immediately willing to do what He wanted. Her only questions were logistical ones. "When and where shall I do this, Lord?" she asked. God answered, "I want you to begin next Wednesday morning at ten o'clock in your home and continue every week as I lead you. I want this house on McCully Street," the Lord said.

"I had never heard of a prayer group in a home, but these were the instructions I received from the Lord and I surely followed them. As the years unfolded, God proved true to His word that He would be in charge of the meetings. No two were ever alike. We invited speakers as He directed, but we didn't announce them ahead of time for God let us know that He wanted people to come, not to hear a certain speaker, but to praise and honor Him."

God gave Tibb further practical instructions. She didn't know that people would come to the prayer group from many churches and denominations, but God knew.

"The Holy Spirit told me that I must never allow anyone

who came to criticize their individual church or minister," Tibb said.

"Isn't that amazing. All of that was given to me, right in my kitchen. But I knew without the slightest doubt that it was indeed the Lord speaking to me and that He intended to lead the meetings in His own way through me."

Tibb needed these specific directions because she was very conventional. She realized that she would have run the meeting like a patterned Methodist meeting if God had not continually reminded her that He was in charge. He didn't want a denominational meeting.

Both Tibb and Dolly thought that many others would be as excited as they were about meeting weekly to talk with God and study the Bible. Tibb invited the women in the Sunday school class she taught at the Mount Lebanon United Methodist Church. She told them about Dolly's miraculous healing and the glorious fellowship they were enjoying with the Lord.

The women listened politely, the blank expressions on their faces provided a barometer of their lack of interest. Tibb understood. It was only a few weeks since she had felt the same way.

"In 1955, people were very suspicious of home prayer groups," Tibb said. "They accepted the home prayer groups that preceded a Billy Graham Crusade, because, in a way, they were church sponsored. I led Methodist prayer meetings sponsored by our church in St. Louis, but these followed a pattern that was familiar to Methodists."

None of these prayer meetings involved prayer for physical healing, and Tibb eventually concluded that Dolly's healing might actually be frightening people. Also, she was telling people that the Holy Spirit would lead the meeting, and as she thought about it, the idea was so new at the time that it probably was intimidating. She was struggling to adjust to this idea herself.

"Many of our friends thought we were fanatical," Tibb said. "I told the Lord I wouldn't worry about what people thought or said about us. Nothing I said or did was going to make people want to come, so I began to relax as the first Wednesday approached."

Six people gathered in Tibb's living room for the first official meeting of what would be known as the Wednesday Morning Prayer Group. Only one woman came from the Methodist Church, and she didn't continue to come for very long. At first, Tibb and Dolly were disappointed, but soon realized that God especially called these first members of the group. Much later, Tibb reflected that God certainly knew better than they did in keeping the group small for a few years.

"We had the experience of Dolly's healing and my spiritual transformation, but we knew very little of the Bible. We had a lot of growing to do before we could be trusted with a large group. God immediately began to act powerfully, and each healing miracle and spiritual transformation in my home taught us valuable lessons about the way He works. God also taught us through the way some people rejected us and chose to ignore our invitation to come to the meetings."

# Chapter 3

## Pot Roast and Hot Apple Pie

> *"For we have heard for ourselves and know that this One is indeed the Savior of the world"* (John 4:42b).

THE SMALL SIZE OF THE NEW PRAYER GROUP IN Tibb's home permitted the women to develop deep and abiding friendships that melded them into a praying fellowship. They did more than pray for needs that came to their attention. Sometimes they took a meal to someone or offered to baby-sit. They visited acquaintances in the hospital and always asked if they could pray before leaving.

Tibb studied the scriptures passionately and applied them to her life before she taught them to the Wednesday group. She didn't teach academically, as she taught pediatric nursing. She taught humbly, as the Holy Spirit began to conform her to the image of Christ. The way she taught the women's Sunday school class changed, too. The change was motivated by her new desire to let the Holy Spirit lead others to Christ through her teaching, rather than to impress anyone with her intellectual gifts.

Backed by the prayers of the small Wednesday group, she withstood the testing of women in the Sunday school class who did not appreciate her new teaching style.

One Sunday morning, her friend Jenny came as close as anyone ever did to drawing an angry response from Tibb. "How did a nurse like you get so much religion?" Jenny asked Tibb. Her question was more taunt than honest inquiry. Her tone showed very little respect for "religion" or for Tibb. In fact, Jenny heckled Tibb from the moment she entered the Sunday school classroom that morning.

Jenny was a feisty little woman who relished a fight. She didn't hesitate to tell everyone about the fights she had with her husband and the way she kept him in line. She thought nothing of interrupting Tibb's Bible lesson in order to make herself the center of attention.

Two dozen women turned their attention from Tibb to Jenny. It was just as well that the women were momentarily distracted, for Tibb was feeling her face flush with a mixture of anger and embarrassment.

Tibb wanted Jenny to know how much Jesus loved her, but she was having trouble getting past her resentment of the woman's rude ways. She was tempted to throw her hands up and ask God why He had inflicted this woman on her. She knew it was important that she demonstrate love to Jenny in this situation, because she represented the Lord Jesus Christ and needed to act as He would act.

In addition, Jenny was one of the few who were showing an interest in coming to the Wednesday Prayer Group "I'll come to your house someday, but I'm going to wait until after Christmas when all the cocktail parties are over," Jenny had told Tibb.

Tibb had replied, "We'll look forward to having you

come," and she had really meant what she said at the time, but this morning, she felt like shaking her.

How could she answer Jenny's mocking question about how she "got religion"? She had told the class about her experience at the Kathryn Kuhlman service. There was no point in telling them again, because they didn't seem to understand that it was more than mere religion that had changed Tibb's life.

What did Jesus do when people in the crowds that followed Him taunted Him and tried to trap Him into saying things they could use against Him?

At that moment, Tibb was certain the Holy Spirit reminded her that Jesus used parables —short stories drawn from life —to confound the mockers. Now is the time for a story, she thought; a story that will illustrate what the power of God can do in a person's life. Let Jenny and the other women find the answer to her question in the story. Tibb called the class back to order and told the following story:

> This is the true story of a woman who wasn't getting along very well with her husband. He was always so busy with some kind of project that he didn't talk, even at the dinner table. When this man was finished eating, he would get up from the table and rush out to the garage where he was doing some lab work. He'd work there until the wee hours of the morning and would never tell his wife what he was doing. It was all a secret.
>
> The dear woman stood the silence as long as she could. Then one day she decided to go to a prayer meeting and ask the pastor to pray for her husband. As the Lord would have it, there happened to be a

very wise minister at the meeting. He studied that woman's face for a while and said to her, "Why did you come today, and what is your problem?"

The lady paused for a moment and then answered, "I don't have a problem, but you can bet your life, my husband has a big problem! He doesn't talk to me anymore. We even eat our dinner in silence. He won't go to church. So I've come to pray for him."

The minister looked at her kindly and asked, "What have you done to please your husband lately?"

"Nothing. Absolutely nothing. Why should I? He doesn't do anything to please me, so I haven't done anything for him. But I'll tell you what I do. Every Sunday I get my Bible under my arm, take my children and walk right out in front of him and go to church. This makes him know that we are Christians, whether he is or not! I just don't care anymore."

The minister looked intently at this dear distraught soul and decided to offer her a little bit of advice. He asked, "What does your husband like to eat?"

"Well,' she said, "I guess his favorite is pot roast and hot apple pie."

"All right," was his reply. "On your way home today, stop at the butcher's and get the best pot roast he has. And also bake a good apple pie for dinner tonight."

"In addition," the minister said, "I'm going to give you a little prayer to memorize, and no matter how discouraged you may become, I want you to pray this prayer often: *Oh, Lord, put your arm around his shoulder, whisper your secrets in his ear, put your love in his heart, and bring him to the ful-*

*fillment of his purpose here on earth."*

So she went home and prayed that prayer. You know, you can't pray without something happening to you. Something always happens to you deep inside. The woman became a little softer, a little sweeter and a little more understanding.

Now the dinner that night was very good, but her husband went right out to his workshop just the same. Even pot roast hadn't led her husband into a conversation. He didn't talk, but she didn't stop praying the prayer the pastor gave her.

Then one day, the praying wife picked up the morning paper. On the front page she read a story about a professor who had made a remarkable discovery in atomic science. Her very own husband was that professor who had brought about the wonderful discovery!

When he came home that evening, she said, "Darling, why didn't you tell me what you were doing? I would have understood."

He told her that it was such a deep secret that he didn't dare to share it with her. Then he told her about a strange thing that had happened to him.

"Do you remember that night when we had the pot roast and hot apple pie?"

She said that she remembered.

"Well," he said, "That night I went out to the garage to work on my experiment the way in which I had been doing it. But I could have sworn that someone placed his arm on my shoulder and said, 'Don't do it that way. Let's try it this new way.'

"I tried it that way and found my answer."

Tibb paused as she finished telling the story to allow the women time to consider what this story might mean in each of their lives.

"Jesus does speak to us, doesn't He? He wants to answer the praying wife's prayer for each one of us and those we love, if we only ask Him, 'Put your arm around *my* shoulder. And whisper your secrets in *my* ear. Put your love in *my* heart and and bring *me* to the fulfillment of *my* purpose here on Earth,'" Tibb said. "How very important it is for each one of us to listen to Jesus and obey Him."

The very next Wednesday after Jenny heard that story, she came to the prayer group. Everyone was surprised, because it was the Wednesday morning *before* Christmas, a Wednesday morning before all the cocktail parties were over.

"And, that very day, Jenny came back to Jesus," Tibb said. "She had accepted Him many years before but told us that she had gotten off the track. That was Jenny—very outspoken and honest, as we all need to be. She told us that she had to leave early that day to go to a cocktail party. She also said, 'I don't know how other people drink in Mount Lebanon, but we drink our liquor in a cup over the sink.'"

Jenny did leave the prayer group early that day to go to her cocktail party. The next Wednesday she came back and told the prayer group all about it. She couldn't understand why all the liquor tasted so horrible to her. Her friends at the party said, "What's happening to you? You're not drinking and you're not the life of the party as you usually are."

"Jenny told them that the Lord had saved her and He had shown her that she had a drinking problem. Jenny told us she wasn't going to drink anymore. That was Jenny. The Lord saved her—her life was changed," Tibb said.

## Pot Roast and Hot Apple Pie

The most dramatic change Jenny told the women about was her new attitude toward her husband, Charlie. She stopped fighting with him and demanding to have her own way. She began to do many things to make him happy. At first he was puzzled, and when he asked what had happened, she told him that she had decided to follow Jesus.

Charlie was so happy about the change that he started to attend church with her, and one day he said to her, "Jenny, do you think you could take me to those praying mantises?" (That was Charlie's name for the prayer group.) Within a short time, he began to attend the prayer group when he wasn't out of town on business.

"Charlie had a complete change of heart," Tibb said. "He began to pray, to read his Bible and was at peace with God. He was quietly excited about his Christian life."

Two years after Charlie went back to church, Tibb made arrangements for Jenny to drive her to a speaking engagement. (Tibb never learned to drive a car.) That morning, Jenny called to tell Tibb that her husband had left early to go on a business trip. While he was at the airport waiting for the plane, he had a heart attack. "Will you go to the hospital with me?" Jenny asked.

Tibb called to cancel her speaking engagement while she waited for Jenny to pick her up. What a surprise they had when they saw Charlie! "We walked into his room and there he was in bed, praying in the name of Jesus," Tibb said. "And when he opened his eyes and saw us, he assured us that everything would be all right, even though he knew that he was dying."

"Before he went to be with the Lord, he told us that had Jenny not found Jesus and brought him to Jesus, he wouldn't be going to heaven."

"So, you see, Jenny made the right choices by coming back to Jesus and giving up alcohol. The change in her life also brought her husband back to the Lord before he died. Our time is, oh, so short. We dare not miss one opportunity to tell people about Jesus," Tibb said.

# Chapter 4
## Peggy, Can You Trust Me?

> "This is the confidence which we have before Him,
> that, if we ask anything according to His will,
> He hears us...we know that we have the requests
> which we have asked from Him" (1 John 5:14-15b).

Peggy G. and her husband, Jim, moved to Pittsburgh from Washington D.C. in 1956. Soon after they moved, she attended a meeting where Tibb Gethin spoke on the power of prayer. "When I was introduced to Tibb after the meeting, I told her that I really believed in prayer," Peggy said. Tibb immediately invited Peggy to attend the prayer group that met in her home every Wednesday morning.

"Now, this wasn't what I had in mind when I mentioned my interest in prayer. Thinking back, I may have been trying to impress Mrs. Gethin with my spirituality. I had become interested in prayer and how it affects people's lives while I was working as Catherine Marshall's secretary. An interest in prayer—a belief in prayer—didn't necessarily mean that I wanted to join a group that actually gathered for the sole purpose of praying," Peggy said.

Peggy invented many excuses that prevented her from

attending. "After about three months, a gentle nudging from God reminded me that it would be a very good idea for me to join the group," Peggy said.

When she finally knocked on Tibb's door on a Wednesday morning, Tibb welcomed her with a hug and the loving statement that she and others had been waiting for Peggy to come. "I was not only accepted but surrounded by love. I felt the support of the group as the months of my first pregnancy slipped by. The prayer and positive input from Tibb's group was important to me because, at the age of thirty-seven, I had some well-meaning friends who warned me that things might not go smoothly for one having a first child at my age.

"Our baby, Jim IV, was born without any problems, and I came home from the hospital happy and excited. I felt that I had done everything right, stayed on my diet, exercised and planned a routine for caring for the baby. I'm sure that I minimized the part that God had in presenting us with the gift of this new life."

Ten days after baby Jim was born, Peggy began having trouble breast-feeding him. The baby was restless and irritable. Peggy wasn't feeling well. She began having difficulty moving her legs, and when she checked her temperature, she found that she had a fever.

"At the suggestion of my family doctor and the gynecologist, I was taken by ambulance to Magee Hospital. There I was subjected to many tests, but none of them revealed what might be wrong with me," Peggy said.

"I was moved to Allegheny General Hospital where the baby had been born, and I was put under the care of an orthopedic surgeon. There were more tests, including a myelogram, and when my temperature soared, nurses applied ice packs to hold down the fever. I was losing muscle strength and was succumbing to a sense of desperation. The doctor decided to operate.

"The day before the operation, Tibb and Bess Rasp, another friend from the prayer group, came to see me and to pray. My husband, Jim, was there to feed me lunch. I had an apparatus attached to the bed so that I could grab the hanging bar to help me lift myself up. Jim had to hold the pipe that was attached to the bed, and it was so hard that his knuckles were white. I felt embarrassed that these women were probably going to pray loud enough for other patients in the room to hear.

"Before she prayed, Tibb asked me if I believed. Believe?! I'd been praying, reading my copy of the daily devotions guide *Upper Room*, and telling God I had a new baby—as if He didn't know—and that I had to get well to take care of the baby.

"'If you believe,' Tibb said, 'then we'll claim this promise in 1 John 5:13: "*I have written this to you who believe in the name of the Son of God, so that you may know that you have eternal life.*"'

"At this point, I remember crying audibly and inside I was thinking, 'Why is Tibb praying about eternal life? I don't want to die. I don't want her to be claiming a promise such as this.'

"And then she went on reading:

*'and this is the confidence which we have before him, that, if we ask anything according to His will, He hears us. And if we know that He hears us in whatever we ask, we know that we have the requests which we have asked from Him'* (1 John 5:14-15).

"After reading the scripture from 1 John, Tibb and Bess offered a short prayer for me, and off they went. They seemed very sure that everything was going to be all right. Jim said, 'That was nice,' but I was still crying. After all, I was the one still lying in bed hurting and unable to move."

The next morning, Jim came to the hospital early to help lift Peggy onto the stretcher to go to the operating room. Sometime during the morning, Tibb called the hospital to find out how Peggy was. When the nurse told Tibb that Peggy was in the operating room, Tibb said, "Oh, I wonder why. She's not going to have an operation today."

"Oh, the faith of the believers!" Peggy said as she recalled how she felt about Tibb's confidence that she would be healed.

Later that day, Peggy came back to the room with bandages around the lower part of her body. She was crying and she said to Jim, "Honey, I don't think they did anything. I still hurt."

Jim consoled Peggy by telling her that the doctor would be coming soon and he would tell them what they had found out when they operated.

The doctor came and said, "We really don't know what's the matter with Peggy. We did some aspirations looking for foreign matter, and we have some blood cultures. But it will take at least forty-eight hours for those to grow. I suggest we pray about this."

"I cried. Jim and the doctor prayed. Then the doctor left the room," Peggy said. "If I could say that there was a flash of lightening, a clap of thunder or an angel at the foot of my bed, it would be dramatic, but it wouldn't be true," she continued.

"Later that afternoon as I lay on the bed, my body felt very heavy. I felt a warm, tingling sensation in my legs and lower body. It seemed to me that a voice was asking,

## Peggy, Can You Trust Me?

'Peggy, can you trust me? Do you know I love you and your baby? Can you give him to me and know that I can take care of him?'

"I felt humbled and afraid. Then I felt very much loved, warmly embraced and so secure that I honestly did not care if I lived or died. I guess I could call it surrendering my will to God," Peggy said.

When Jim came back that evening, he told Peggy about a strange experience he had on the way to the hospital. "As I swung onto the parkway, it was like I heard a voice, felt a presence in the car and knew within myself that you were better," Jim said. He also knew that when he walked in the room, Peggy would say "Jimmy, honey, I'm feeling better."

As Jim walked into Peggy's hospital room, she called out to him across the room, "Jimmy, honey, I'm feeling better."

Jim ran over to the bed and said, "Peggy, I knew you were going to say that." He had tears in his eyes and he added, "God is really in this thing with us."

Later, X rays showed that Peggy's sacroiliac bone had been damaged by infection, but by September, three months after the baby was born, the bone was healing and fusing back together. By October, she was able to give up the walker she had been using.

"I dared share with the doctor that I thought God had something to do with the specific change that day in the hospital and that He was responsible for my healing," Peggy said. "The doctor agreed and assured me that I was correct in my assumptions. He acknowledged that he was present at the exploratory surgery but he hadn't done anything.

"I praise the Lord and thank Him constantly for my son and for my good health. The day that Tibb prayed for me in the hospital, something I learned from Catherine Marshall became real to me," said Peggy.

"The answers to prayer aren't the most important thing about talking with God. The most important aspect of prayer is building a relationship between the pray-er and God."

# Chapter 5
## The Blessing of the Gold Box

> *"Test Me now in this,"* says the LORD of hosts,
> *"if I will not open for you the windows
> of heaven and pour out for you a blessing
> until it overflows"* (Malachi 3:10b).

PEGGY G. WAS HEALED A FEW WEEKS BEFORE THE prayer group's first anniversary. It wasn't an instantaneous healing. God set the healing process in motion and within three months, the healing of her damaged sacroiliac was completed.

Dolly was healed instantly so that was what the group expected when they prayed for healing. The women in the prayer group learned through Peggy's experience that God exercises His gifts of healing in more than one way. In fact, over the years, they learned that each healing was different and tailored to the needs of the individual.

Peggy's sister, Rosemary, was impressed with the way God healed Peggy and she began to come to the prayer group. She and her husband moved to Pittsburgh when he was accepted into The University of Pittsburgh Medical School. They had a baby and hadn't lived in the city very long when her husband was diagnosed with tuberculosis and couldn't work.

"He had to go to a sanatorium, and although we prayed, he wasn't healed immediately. We asked the Lord what we should do for them during this difficult period," Tibb said. "The Lord answered through prayer that we were to undergird their rent and whatever they needed to buy food.

"At that time, we weren't a very large group and we didn't take offerings. We just set out a box someone had covered with gold paper and the person who was appointed treasurer would let us know when there was enough money in the box to send out a donation. Then, we would pray about who should receive the money.

"From the time the Lord let us know that we should help Rosemary and her husband, the treasurer would open the box each week and find enough money to pay the couple's expenses. These were cash donations, and no one ever knew how much anyone else gave, but the Lord brought the money in.

"An amazingly short time later, Rosemary's husband called her to say that he was being released from the sanitarium early and that he knew the process of healing had been shortened by our prayers. He was so relieved to have a home to go to and was very grateful for all the group had done."

That's how the gold box became another way that God taught the group about His power to direct individuals to accomplish His purpose. As time went on, the group was able to support other people and groups, when led to do so through prayer. Sometimes they heard about needs through speakers. The late Anglican bishop of Kigezi Diocese, Kabale, Uganda, Festo Kivengere, was one of those speakers with

## The Blessing of the Gold Box

whom they had a continuing relationship. It involved giving money to *African Enterprise*, a mission he extended into East Africa where the Holy Spirit poured out His power. Festo came to the prayer group when he was in the Pittsburgh area studying at a local seminary. He was a classmate of Dr. Patrick Albright, who later became pastor of the Mount Lebanon United Methodist Church where Tibb was a member.

When Festo came to the prayer group, he told the remarkable story of his conversion during a period of powerful activity of the Holy Spirit in East Africa. At that time, his sister attended the Anglican Church in his hometown where she became a Christian. Through the intercessory prayers of that church, Festo was led to give his life to the Lord.

His conversion came about in an unusual way. One day, Festo's sister, who was sitting near the front of the church in their homeland, spoke out in the church and said she felt led to say that Festo would come to Jesus that day. Now, unbeknownst to her, Festo had slipped into the back of the church, and when he heard what she said, he left in a hurry and took off across the countryside on his motorbike. He had no intention of becoming a Christian that day—or any other day.

At that time, he was running around with a fast crowd and he was a heavy drinker and rabble-rouser. As he rode down a country road, miles from anywhere, he saw an old friend with whom he'd had a falling out. The friend motioned for him to stop and immediately asked him for forgiveness for causing the incident over which they'd fought.

Now, Festo knew he himself had incited the incident, and he wanted to know why his estranged friend was seeking forgiveness. The friend told him that Jesus had forgiven all his sins and he felt obligated to ask forgiveness of all those he had offended.

## The House on McCully Street

God used his friend to lance the wound of Festo's unforgiving spirit that had been eating him up for years. As a small child, the young African, his sister and mother, had witnessed the martyrdom of his father. It was during the years that an outlaw group was terrorizing the area, and they came to the family's home and herded them into a bedroom where they hung and then dismembered the father while the family watched.

Festo and the others were on their knees praying and begging for mercy when the terrorists finished with his father. One of them approached the mother with the intention of killing her, too. The other outlaws shook their heads and walked away saying, "No more killing." Despite the fact that God answered their prayers and spared their lives, Festo couldn't forgive the men who had murdered his father.

Unforgiveness burned in his heart and he turned away from God, until the day his friend providentially met him on the road and asked for forgiveness. Festo was so touched by God's love through his friend that he gave his heart to the Lord right there on the road. Immediately, he turned his bike around and traveled back to the church. You must remember that these East African church services were lengthy and people were still there worshipping God when Festo arrived back at the church several hours after he left. Everyone received his testimony with great joy.

Festo's mother attended a Christian conference when she was very old, and a man came and introduced himself to her as the man who had killed her husband. He had become a Christian, and with tears, begged her to forgive him. She answered without hesitation, "I forgave you when you did it." She could only do this in the power of the Holy Spirit.

## The Blessing of the Gold Box

Many women at the prayer group cried when they heard Festo's story. They were learning that the body of Christ, His church, extends to the far corners of the earth and that others are not as blessed as we are in America. They learned that Christians in other lands suffer beyond what we can imagine in our sheltered lives. God was teaching them compassion and giving them a model for forgiveness.

"Gifts [of the Holy Spirit] are wonderful, and we rejoice when people are healed," one of the women in the prayer group said. "But I think what we need more than anything else is the power of the Spirit to forgive. Who has not experienced the pain of an unforgiving spirit?"

God was preparing them to meet Ruby Haff, a woman whose unforgiving spirit was warping all her relationships and very likely was a factor in the crippling arthritis she had when she came to the group for the first time.

# Chapter 6
## A Paralyzing Hatred

> *"But if you do not forgive others,
> then your Father will not forgive your
> transgressions"* (Matthew 6:15).

THE FIRST TIME RUBY HAFF CAME TO THE PRAYER group, her perfectly fitted sheath dress was accessorized with a beautiful flowered hat and white gloves. Ruby was a very handsome woman, and her style was memorable. She had been a Baptist all her life and had heard Tibb speak at the Mount Lebanon Baptist Church where she was a member. No one knew from her appearance and jaunty manner that she hated her father and was unable to forgive him for the terrible way he had treated her as a child.

She and her husband, Jack, moved from place to place quite often. She made a point of joining a church every time they moved. Yet, each time they moved, she was disappointed within herself that her faith seemed like a light at the end of a tunnel and she wasn't moving any closer to that light. She wanted something to happen that would move her closer to that light. But she didn't know what to do. She didn't realize that her hatred for her father was holding her back from all that she wanted. Her father was an alcoholic, and as far back as she could remember, he had made her life miserable.

"The hatred had a grip on Ruby, and that hatred went into every church right along with her," Tibb said. "As a result, she never could be released into the joy the Lord had for her."

Ruby was apprehensive about coming to the prayer group that first morning, but she felt like she was surrounded by a warm blanket of love. No one seemed to notice that she was overdressed for the occasion, and the women invited her to share their brown-bag lunches. Tibb listened to the small talk from the perspective of what a stranger might think of their trivial chit-chat.

"We were all good friends and chattered like magpies. I wondered what Ruby might think about the talk. Among other things, Jenny's husband had died several years before and she was talking very frankly about a new romance.

"When the lunch was over and Ruby was leaving, she said she was very relieved that we weren't a 'holier than thou' bunch and she'd like to come back."

She came regularly, and a few weeks later, Tibb read the story of the rich young ruler from the third chapter of the Gospel of John to the assembled group:

> *Now there was a man of the Pharisees, named Nicodemus, a ruler of the Jews; this man came to Jesus by night and said to Him, "Rabbi, we know that You have come from God as a teacher; for no one can do these signs that You do unless God is with him." Jesus answered and said to him, "Truly, truly, I say to you, unless one is born again he cannot see the*

## A Paralyzing Hatred

*kingdom of God." Nicodemus said to Him 'How can a man be born when he is old? He cannot enter a second time into his mother's womb and be born, can he?'"* (John 3:1-4).

Tibb's face was radiant when she read the scripture, and at this point in the reading, she paused for commentary. "Was it not evidence of the man's sincerity that he asked such a childlike question?" she asked. "And we see the magnificent way in which Jesus captured the heart of the man by first capturing his attention. The man was probably picturing the birth of a child in his mind, and the question sprang from his mouth spontaneously—How could a man be born when he is old?

"Aren't you sitting there in your chair with a similar thought in your mind? How can this be? What a strange thing for Jesus to say.

"Now that Jesus had the man's full attention," she continued, "he began to explain that a second birth is a spiritual birth."

Tibb read more of the story from the Bible:

*Jesus answered, "Truly, truly, I say to you, unless one is born of water and the Spirit he cannot enter into the kingdom of God. That which is born of the flesh is flesh, and that which is born of the Spirit is spirit. Do not be amazed that I said to you, 'You must be born again.' The wind blows where it wishes and you hear the sound of it, but do not know where it comes from and where it is going; so is everyone who is born of the Spirit'"* (John 3:5-8).

She paused to observe the response of the listeners. Then she explained that a Jew like Nicodemus would have heard of the water baptism of John the Baptist. And he would also know the books of Moses and the prophets that form the Old Testament.

"In the Old Testament, the Holy Spirit came upon the prophets from time to time for special activities He needed them to do," Tibb said. "Now, when we acknowledge we are sinners and invite Jesus to be our redeemer—the One who saves us from our sin —His Holy Spirit comes to live in our hearts permanently. The scriptures say that we are baptized in the Holy Spirit, who then begins to transform our lives.

"Being 'born again' is a matter of admitting that you are a sinner—no matter how good you think you are, because God requires perfection. You know that no one is perfect except Jesus Christ, who is God made manifest in flesh," Tibb said.

"If you confess that Jesus is Lord and invite him to be Lord of your life, then you are immediately born again by the will of God the Father. He adopts you into His family. You become a child of God."

Ruby committed her life to the Lord Jesus Christ that morning. Tibb told her that she was born again. Later, Ruby told Tibb that God spoke to her as she drove home on that special day. He told her to write a letter to her father telling him what had happened to her. So she wrote the letter that night.

"Daddy," Ruby wrote, "I have found Jesus in a wonderful, new, living way. You don't have to belong to a church, Daddy. All you to have to do is get down on your knees and ask God to forgive you. He will come into your heart. He'll do it, Daddy."

She sent the letter to him, but the mailman never brought a reply to her letter. Time went by. Then one day,

## A Paralyzing Hatred

her mother called on the phone. Her mother said, "Ruby, your Daddy committed his life to Jesus today and joined the Baptist church."

As long as Tibb lived, she loved to tell and retell the story of the chain reaction that God set in motion when Ruby was born again. When she came to the point in the story when Ruby found out that her father had accepted Christ as a result of her letter, Tibb always paused to let others experience her own joy as the story unfolded.

"Oh, how Ruby did rejoice when her mother told her the good news that her father had received Jesus as his Savior," Tibb said. "It was just two years after Ruby came to Jesus that her father came, too. Very shortly after that, the Lord took him home. Ruby said that if she had not given up that resentment and released her father into the Lord's hands, these things couldn't have happened. How right she was.

"Along with the resentment Ruby had felt, that dear precious woman had developed arthritis. Her joints were terribly swollen, and she was in constant pain. It hurt us all to see her suffer so much, for everyone in the group loved Ruby. But once again, the Holy Spirit was faithful and healed Ruby during a Kathryn Kuhlman healing service." Following the Kathryn Kuhlman service, Tibb took Ruby to visit her Aunt Janet who lived in Tionesta, north of Pittsburgh.

"Aunt Janet's prayer group was meeting that day, and although Ruby sat still for a long time, she had no pain whatsoever," Tibb said. "She had had this pain for a good many years, and unlike some of the others, Miss Kuhlman didn't call out the healing and Ruby didn't feel anything unusual at the time. It was while she sat there at my Aunt Janet's prayer group that she was positive her Lord and

## The House on McCully Street

Savior had truly healed her. The pain didn't return, and as long as we met in my home, Ruby's cane sat in the corner of the dining room."

Shortly after God healed Ruby, she became Tibb's assistant at the Wednesday morning meetings.

"Somehow the Lord always assigned the people to help me. I never selected anyone by myself," Tibb said. "At the same time that He spoke to me about Ruby's leadership, He spoke to Ruby as well, so that God's direction was confirmed in both our hearts.

"We must all be so careful to really listen when He speaks, for He is the best father that any of us will ever have to direct our path in this world."

Although many people think of Tibb Gethin as a healer —one whose prayers led to physical healing of illness and affliction—Tibb believed that she was first called to be an evangelist. No one this side of heaven will ever know the number of those she led to salvation through Jesus Christ and the way in which they, too, witnessed to an ever-widening circle of family, friends and acquaintances.

# Chapter 7

## *Answers to Three Prayers*

> *And a woman who had been suffering from a hemorrhage for twelve years, came up behind Him and touched the fringe of His cloak; for she was saying to herself, "If I only touch His garment, I will get well"* (Matthew 9:20,21).

A NURSE FROM PRESBYTERIAN HOSPITAL CALLED Tibb one day and she said her name was Helen. She wondered if there really was a prayer meeting in Tibb's home in Mount Lebanon every week, and Tibb assured her that there was. She was pleased to hear that Tibb was a nurse, too.

Then she said, "I have three weeks off, and I'd like to come to the prayer meeting to have prayer for a problem. Is it possible to have prayer for the problem without telling what the problem is?"

Tibb told her that the group prayed for many unspoken concerns and people reported that God answered these prayers.

Helen had another concern. She was afraid to pray out loud and wondered if she would feel embarrassed if she didn't pray out loud. Tibb assured her that she wouldn't feel embarrassed if she didn't pray aloud. Helen said that she would definitely come the following Wednesday.

"It was a pleasure to see that beautiful, tall young woman when she walked in the door that first week," Tibb said. "She sat next to me on my right, and when we were ready to pray, she whispered to me, 'Tibb, are you going to call on me to pray out loud?' 'No,' I said once again.

"Isn't it amazing how self-conscious people are about praying out loud? It's only until they meet Jesus, and then it's just a matter of having a conversation with Him."

When the group prayer began, Tibb was amazed when one of the first voices she heard praying came from her right. It was Helen. "It was a beautiful prayer of thanksgiving, welcoming the Lord and honoring Jesus. It was just beautiful!" Tibb said.

After the meeting was finished, Helen said, "Tibb, were you surprised that I was praying?" Tibb said that she was very surprised. "Well," the nurse said, "Right here in this living room, Jesus appeared before me with His hands outstretched. I saw Him and I had to thank Him for being here with us." That was Helen's "born again" experience, and no one was surprised when she came back the following week.

"Helen hadn't mentioned a physical problem," Tibb recalled. "The meeting was practically over the second week, and Helen was sitting on the chair between the dining room and living room.

"I looked over at her and was amazed to see her face and neck turning red. The others saw me looking at her and turned to look, too. We all saw a lump disappearing from her neck. It was a large lump, but we hadn't noticed it until it turned red. Helen told us later that the doctors wouldn't operate on it because surgery might have damaged her vocal

## Answers to Three Prayers

chords. So she decided to let well enough alone."

Tears were streaming down her cheeks as the lump disappeared. She ran into the powder room and looked at herself in the mirror. "It's gone. It's gone," she said. The lump had disappeared completely and a visit to her doctor revealed that there was no trace of it.

"All we need is the presence of the living, healing Christ in our midst. That is all we ever need," said Tibb.

The third week, Helen was back once again. She whispered to Tibb, "I haven't received the answer to my unspoken request yet."

"Just keep on praying," Tibb said to Helen.

The meeting ended, and everyone went home. Later that afternoon, the telephone rang and it was Helen.

"Tibb, you'll never believe it! You'll never believe it!"

"Oh, yes, I will," Tibb answered.

Helen told Tibb that the unspoken request was for her husband. He had been trying to obtain a promotion in his company. He had felt certain that he would get it, and then the company hired a younger man from New York to take the job. She said her husband had become so bitter that they were getting on each other's nerves at home. They were both very discouraged, and that was the secret reason she had come to the prayer group.

"Today my husband called me to say that they sent the other fellow back to New York and gave my husband the job!" The excitement in her voice was equal to the excitement she showed when her first two prayer requests were answered."

Helen came for only three Wednesdays, and each week she received the answer to her prayer. The answers were dramatic and memorable, but the direction for the prayer group that Tibb received through these answers was even more significant.

"Through Helen's experience, God showed me the most important ministries the prayer group would have in the future," Tibb said. "God would use us to lead people to personal salvation; in healing of the body and in reconciliation between husbands and wives. It was clear direction, and it helped me to be firm in keeping the group focused on God's purpose for us.

# Chapter 8
## Stand Up and Walk

> *"Then I will make up to you for the years That the swarming locust has eaten..."* (Joel 2:25a).

TIBB NEVER SUGGESTED THAT ANYONE STOP taking their medication when they came to the prayer group expecting God to heal them. She believed that God initiated every medical advance that researchers and doctors make and He does this to benefit mankind.

She especially remembered Peggy Hoffman and the dramatic healing she received from God in Tibb's living room. Peggy had been an invalid for eight years, and during that time she had availed herself of every medical means available. Following a healing service she attended before she came to the Wednesday Prayer Group, Peggy believed that God wanted her to stop taking the medicine she had been taking for a good many years with no appreciable change in her condition. Her family supported her in this decision because her situation was so desperate.

Tibb recalled that Vivian Thompson, a practical nurse who was one of the six original members of the prayer group, brought Peggy to the group. At the time, Peggy had exhausted every medical treatment available with no relief, and when she gave up the medicine, new complications developed.

"I'll never forget how those women received me with love," Peggy said. "I surely was no prize to look at. Soon after George and I were married, I was diagnosed with a terrible muscular condition called dermatomyositis. It's in the same family of diseases as multiple sclerosis, and it was as difficult to live with as the name is to pronounce."

She felt better after the birth of the couple's first child, Forrest, and for a short time, they believed that she was recovering. But, soon the disease became worse. She lost her sense of balance, and her muscles became progressively weaker. Then she developed a skin condition that caused her whole body to swell.

"My eyes were practically swollen shut, and this swelling was accompanied by unbearable itching."

During that period of time, she spent three months in the University of Pennsylvania Hospital in Philadelphia, undergoing a multitude of tests followed by diagnoses. Then, she returned to Pittsburgh, where she spent another three months in the hospital. Finally, she was discharged to go home.

"In spite of medication, I had no relief from the symptoms. My mother cared for me and for my son," she said. "How I grieved that I couldn't take care of my dear little boy, and I thought my heart would break when my mother took him to school on his first day.

"Through it all, I thanked God for my loving family. They all upheld me tenaciously with such a strong faith.

They assured me that God doesn't distinguish between curable and incurable diseases, as men call them. They prayed that God would heal me as they took care of me, for I was helpless without them."

Peggy's family recognized that she was reaching the end of her endurance, and in an effort to find relief for her, they took her to a healing service at a nearby church. During the evening, the minister stopped the service and described Peggy's condition in minute detail.

"I believe that God revealed my need to that minister, and he called out for the young woman whose condition he described to come forward. What a moment that was. He had never seen me before, and he was proclaiming a miracle on my behalf," Peggy said.

She stood to her feet, and as she acknowledged the healing, a Bible verse from the book of James flowed into her mind: *"The effectual fervent prayer of a righteous man availeth much"* (James 5:16b, KJV). "Then I knew that Jesus was speaking another verse to me: *'This kind can come forth by nothing, but by prayer and fasting'* (Mark 9:29, KJV). I told my family the verse God gave me, and they immediately assured me that they would fast and pray with me for my healing."

Peggy stopped taking all the medication the doctors had prescribed in response to another Bible verse she believes God gave her, *"Therefore I say to you, all things for which you pray and ask, believe that you have received them, and they will be granted you"* (Mark 11:24). "We prayed and believed that God wanted me to exercise faith by giving up the medicine," she said.

Huge boils broke out over her entire body three different times. Improvement was very slow, and she had many setbacks. She slipped into a deep despair. But her husband, George, and her mother never wavered in their faith.

God continued to bring passages of scripture to her mind, and in the deep emotional pit in which she found herself, God reminded her of another verse that strengthened her: *"Yet, with respect to the promise of God, he did not waver in unbelief, but grew strong in faith, giving glory to God"* (Romans 4:20).

She was encouraged by this promise, and it was soon after God gave her this verse that Vivian told her about the Wednesday Prayer Group and offered to take her. Peggy attended for several weeks, and although the women prayed fervently for her, she wasn't healed right away. "Then, one Wednesday morning, it happened. In one moment, it happened. The whole group was really deep in prayer," Peggy recalled.

"The Lord told Tibb that I was to stand up and that I was healed. Well, for the first time in many years, I stood up, miraculously, with no effort and no pain. What a beautiful, beautiful miracle. Then, right away everyone joyfully sang, 'Praise God From Whom All Blessings Flow.' It was a day and a hymn that many of us will never forget."

This happened in 1956, about a year after the prayer meetings began, and Peggy has been healthy ever since. "I've seen God work in miraculous ways in my life since that wonderful day, and I know Christ's healing love was there in that home in a unique way," Peggy said.

"In addition to my illness, the doctor told me I'd never have any more children. They were wrong. After I was healed, the Lord blessed George and me with three lovely, healthy daughters."

When she reflects upon the years that she and her family persevered in prayer during her years of trial and the blessings that followed, another Bible verse became very special to her:

*And I will restore to you the years that the locust hath eaten, the cankerworm, and the caterpiller, and the palmerworm, my great army which I sent among you. And ye shall eat in plenty, and be satisfied, and praise the name of the LORD your God, that hath dealt wondrously with you: and my people shall never be ashamed* (Joel 2:25-26, KJV).

# Chapter 9

## *A Wednesday Dose of Love*

> *We give thanks to God always for all of you, making mention of you in our prayers; constantly bearing in mind your work of faith and labor of love...* (1 Thessalonians 1:2-3).

THE PRAYER GROUP WAS FIVE YEARS OLD IN 1960, and Tibb began to realize the wonderful diversity of people God was bringing into the group. The original six were middle-class women of similar backgrounds. Within five years, those who came were people of various economic levels, church affiliations and ethnic backgrounds. She also noticed that a growing number of men were coming and many of them were pastors. When she thought about Bob Caldwell, a pastor who began to come regularly in 1960, she called him her anniversary gift.

Bob Caldwell was the pastor of a church about thirty miles south of Pittsburgh, and a friend told him about Tibb's prayer ministry. When he accepted the responsibility of organizing two weekend prayer emphasis seminars in his community, he invited her to come, and he also invited a group of men from The Pittsburgh Experiment. Sam Shoemaker, an Episcopalian pastor, started the Pittsburgh Experiment in 1955 with a small group of businessmen. This group was growing during the same period of time that the Wednesday Prayer Group began to flourish.

Tibb was gaining a reputation for her ability to capture the attention of an audience with Bible stories and anecdotes that communicated deep spiritual truth. Bob invited her to bring some of the ladies from the prayer group with her.

He recalls that it was a very cold Friday when they came, and they all were wearing their fur coats and boots.

"It was a bit unusual to see so many women so dressed up in our rural area," Bob said.

"Tibb and the others with her spoke to the group about Jesus, the power of prayer and the importance of daily Bible reading. They also came back the next day, Saturday, with more Bible teaching about a personal relationship with Jesus," Bob said.

"We had two different meetings in two different churches—one for women and one for men. The two days were a real success, and people in our area were greatly influenced by the teaching." As a result of this meeting with Tibb, Bob began to attend the Wednesday prayer meetings in her home.

"I was inspired by these meetings, primarily because I felt so much love from the very first day that Tibb welcomed me. I knew the Holy Spirit was there in a way I hadn't experienced before and that was something I wanted. For years I prayed that I might be a channel for God's love as Tibb and her group were."

Tibb often said that God gave her His gift of love the day Dolly was healed. Others might covet more dramatic

## A Wednesday Dose of Love

gifts from God, but she was content to disburse God's love to everyone she met. She was a model for those who attended the Wednesday group, and they, too, became special channels for God's love.

Bob, like many people in pastoral roles, kept his own counsel. How can a pastor confide his personal problems to members of his congregation? Bob knew he had as many prayer needs as anyone in his congregation, but he was reluctant to ask for prayer in his own church.

Over a period of years, as he made the trip to Tibb's for his weekly dose of love, the Lord was breaking down the barriers that kept him from openness about his own life and personal spiritual needs. It was many years before he felt comfortable enough with them to tell the prayer group about his relationship with his father.

"I had been estranged from my father for about forty years, and God knew how important it was for me to share my story." Bob said.

"It was important to me, and it was important to Ruby Haff, who was standing behind me as I told my story. She was crying her heart out because she had gone through a similar experience with her father. God taught us similar lessons through alcoholic fathers.

"God's timing is always perfect, and when I related details of my life, Pastor Albert Steiner and his wife Ava helped me to understand the act of forgiving. They had dealt with bitterness themselves and often helped people understand the importance of forgiveness.

"Ava said that forgiveness is not an emotion, it's an act of obedience to God. Ruby and I both learned to approach personal forgiveness with a picture of Christ on the cross forgiving those who put Him there."

When Bob retired in 1989, he and his wife, Frances, invited the prayer group members to attend a retirement party in his church.

"I was thrilled to have so many of them come, and I was overwhelmed when Tibb told me that she never saw so much love from a congregation for their pastor," Bob said.

"One of the hardest things I ever had to do was to leave the Wednesday Morning Prayer Group when we moved away. Visits are still possible, and what rejoicing, love and inspiration is in store for us each time we renew our friendships.

"Tibb's group prepared me to grow in faith and receive blessings from the Lord that I might have passed by. My life was blessed for almost thirty years by the fellowship of these sisters and brothers in the Lord."

# Chapter 10
## Saved by Grace

*For by grace you have been saved through faith; and that not of yourselves, it is the gift of God, not as a result of works, so that no one may boast* (Ephesians 2:8-9).

Betty Overend came to the Wednesday Prayer Group for the first time in 1961. She came with a friend who knew that Betty was feeling dissatisfied with her spiritual life.

Betty remembers how surprised she was to see so many people at a prayer meeting and even more surprised when the group singing began. She enjoyed singing, and her heart was strangely warmed by the Bible teaching. She decided to come back the following week. The second week, Tibb asked Betty to stay after the meeting.

"I sat in a blue chair, and Tibb talked to me about a personal relationship with Jesus Christ," Betty said. "I was very active in a local church and thought that belonging to a church and living a good life was the sum and substance of spirituality.

"She told me how much God loved me and that He sent His Son Jesus to die on the cross for my sins."

### The House on McCully Street

Tibb explained to Betty that she couldn't earn her salvation with good works.

"It's a free gift," Tibb told her and quoted two verses from Ephesians 2: "*For by grace you have been saved through faith, and that not of yourselves, it is a gift of God; not as a result of works; that no one should boast.*"

Betty believed what Tibb said was true. She immediately asked Tibb to pray with her as she committed her life to Christ and invited the Holy Spirit to direct her life.

"Some people give their lives to Christ and they don't feel differently right away, but I felt like I was walking on a cloud. I felt kind of glowy as I left the meeting, and I still felt that way when I got home," Betty said.

She wondered how she could explain to her husband, Joe, what had happened to her that morning. For many years, she and the couple's five children attended church while Joe spent his Sunday mornings at the golf course. When he did begin attending church, he became very active, and she knew he believed that he could work his way to heaven.

When Joe got home from work that day, he noticed right away that Betty seemed different. She had a kind of radiance about her that he'd never noticed before. He encouraged her to tell him about her day, and she immediately started to talk about a prayer meeting where somebody named Tibb had prayed for her.

"I sat in a blue chair, and Tibb told me that good works weren't going to get me into heaven and that I needed Jesus," Betty said.

She knew she was talking very fast and trying to explain her experience before Joe could interrupt. When she told him she had invited Jesus into her heart, he wasn't sure what that meant. He had always assumed that God

*Saved by Grace*

accepted them because they were such good people and they worked so hard in the church.

Joe felt pretty satisfied with himself. He had progressed from dropping the children off for Sunday school and "communing with nature" on the golf course to going to church with Betty and the children, taking on a lot of maintenance projects around the building and serving on the elder board. He remembered only too well when his daughter asked him why he didn't come into the church with her.

"When I tried to tell her about 'communing with nature,' it sounded kind of lame, and I decided I better go to church," Joe said. "Now, here I was again, after all the progress I'd made, and I felt like I did when I tried to explain 'communing with nature' to my daughter."

Betty wanted him to come to the prayer meeting so that he, too, could have a personal relationship with Jesus. Although he saw the change in Betty—she continued to glow with a kind of inner light that he couldn't explain—and he was drawn to her description of the free gift of salvation, he didn't want to go to a prayer meeting where he might be the only man. He began to pray in the best way he knew how, and it was a simple prayer: "God, if this personal relationship is what I need, tell me how to get it."

"I'll never forget the way God spoke to me when I prayed," Joe said. "It was so clear, I knew this inner voice was God answering my prayer. God said, 'Son, when you're ready, I'm ready.' How do I get ready? How do I get closer to you?" Joe asked God.

Not long after Joe asked this important question, friends invited him and his wife to go to a Kathryn Kuhlman meeting. At that service, Joe heard there was nothing he could do to get ready for heaven except to trust in the sacrificial death of Christ on the cross and His resurrection that followed three days later.

Miss Kuhlman talked about God's plan of salvation, and it broke Joe's heart to know that Jesus had to die to pay the price for his sin. His heart was filled with gratitude.

"Yes, Lord," Joe thought to himself, "Now I'm ready." If Betty glowed after she accepted Jesus as her Savior and Lord, Joe exploded with energy in his quest to take the gospel to others. He wanted to go to the Wednesday Prayer Group, and when he heard the beautiful singing, he understood why Betty loved the joyful worship. He also found that there were enough men coming that he didn't feel like a loner.

"The first time I came to the prayer group, Tibb was in a wheelchair and I thought to myself, 'What is the head angel doing in a wheelchair?'" Joe recalled.

Before he left the meeting that day, he would have the answer to his unspoken question.

"At the end of the meeting, Tibb invited anyone with special prayer needs to come to the altar for prayer. Then she motioned for me to push her wheelchair over to a man who was standing in one of the side aisles like he was waiting for someone. Tibb told me that she believed this guy, John, was ready to commit his life to Christ and she wanted to talk to him about it," Joe said. Joe left the two together. Later, Tibb told him John's story.

John's wife, Boots, didn't drive, so John had been driving her to the prayer group for several years. He never came in. He would spend the two hours doing errands or he would read or sleep in the car.

John was an army engineer and a Roman Catholic. He never objected to Boots coming, nor did he ever complain about the distance he had to drive, but for himself, he just wasn't sure it was the place for him until God arranged a series of events that changed his mind.

Tibb always looked forward to a Christmas tea that Jean Yocum hosted for the group every year. She asked Carol Nomides to invite John to the party.

"I'll see," John said.

John waited outside during the prayer meeting the day of the party, but he drove Boots to Jean's home and went to the party. He told Boots that he had a very good time and felt comfortable with the people. The following week, he parked the car at the church and went to the prayer meeting. It was the second time John went that Tibb asked Joe Overend to wheel her over to talk with him.

"There was nothing Tibb liked better than telling the stories of how God worked his miracles of bringing people into His family," Joe said. "God gifted her to know that John was ready to receive Christ that day.

"She told me that she was very direct when she spoke to John. 'The Lord is calling your name,' Tibb said to John, and he replied, 'I know,'" said Joe.

"Tibb asked him if he was ready to accept Jesus as his Lord and Savior, and he said, 'Yes, Ma'am.' Tibb led him through the sinner's prayer of repentance, and he accepted Jesus immediately," said Joe.

That same day, Tibb stepped out of her wheelchair, healed of the affliction the doctor said would confine her to the chair the rest of her life. Tibb called her healing a gift of God for herself and for those two men, John and Joe, who were encouraged when they saw God's power at work healing Tibb.

Joe and Betty Overend picked up many responsibilities in the prayer group and became very close friends with Tibb and her husband, Wynn. The four of them had wonderful times together, and following Wynn's death, the Overends were a continuing support to Tibb in the leadership of the prayer group.

## Chapter 11
## *All Things Work Together for Good*

"*And they were all filled with the Holy Spirit and began to speak with other tongues, as the Spirit was giving them utterance*" (Acts 2:4).

T IBB COULD IDENTIFY WITH JOE AND BETTY'S IDEA that they could satisfy God with their good works. Prior to Dolly's healing, she had only a modest knowledge of the scriptures and shared their idea that she could gain God's approval by her good works. She was a good person who was steeped in the virtues learned from her godly parents and regular attendance at Sunday school and church. She didn't know that God wanted to direct her life through the Holy Spirit until the night Dolly was healed and she received what she called a baptism of love from the Holy Spirit.

She studied the Bible to learn more about what she experienced the day Dolly was healed, but it didn't take her long to know that she would never fully grasp the way God had entered her life with this new power to live her life according to His will. She knew her job was to act on what she was learning as she studied. She soon recognized that her focus on personal salvation and using the gifts of the Spirit as Kathryn Kuhlman did was as likely to alienate people as it was to win them.

As she learned more about the various gifts of the Spirit and God exercised them through her, she saw former friends turn away from her. Believing that God had called her to be a channel for His love, she continued to relate to them without resentment. She focused on the fact that the Holy Spirit gives Christians the power to live holy lives in accordance with what the Bible teaches. If she exercised the Holy Spirit's gift of evangelism, she also concentrated on the next step—a disciplined devotional life.

"How can anyone follow Christ and become more like Him if they don't study the Bible for direction? So many Christians are stunted in their growth because they don't come to Him daily in Bible study and prayer," Tibb said.

"The physical and emotional problems people shared with us seemed secondary to their need to fully commit their lives to a loving God and grow to maturity in their faith through daily Bible reading and prayer."

Her meeting with Ava Steiner was confirmation that the prayer group needed to focus on the saving grace of Jesus Christ if she was to fulfill her mission as a spiritual pediatrician. Others might be led by God to focus their ministry on the gifts of the Spirit, but she was called to teach obedience to basic Christian principles.

Tibb met Ava Steiner at a spiritual life conference in Mount Lebanon, and Ava told her how she and her husband were grievously hurt by the controversy surrounding their use of the gifts of the Holy Spirit. The Steiners expected to be career missionaries and loved working among people who lived in a small Texas town near the Mexican border. They had served there for sixteen years when an unusual experience alienated them from their sponsoring missionary organization.

"The first term Albert started an elementary school," Ava said, "The second term he established a boarding high school. We were thrilled to be able to begin each class with prayer and see children blossom as they gained new skills."

Ava was teaching typing in the high school when God interrupted her lesson plan for the day.

"During prayer time with the students before I started the lesson, a thought came to my mind so strongly that I felt compelled to speak out.

She said, "Someone has an unspoken prayer request and I want to encourage you to pray aloud and God will answer."

She asked everyone to keep their heads bowed and to allow God to prompt them to pray aloud. Almost immediately, she heard a young man begin to pray. At first, he spoke with quavering voice and then his words became strong with conviction.

"I am bound by a spirit of envy," the young man prayed. "Please set me free."

Ava was stunned by the fervor of the prayer and she believes that God inspired her response.

"You must denounce this spirit of envy in the name of the Lord Jesus Christ," she said. "For Jesus taught His disciples to denounce the works of Satan and cling to Him, for He loves you and came to this earth to redeem His children from sin."

Her mind was flooded with scriptures that demonstrated the awful consequences of acting out of an envious spirit. The story of Joseph sold into slavery by envious brothers left no shadow of doubt in her mind that envy was a work of Satan.

She spoke with authority, using words from James, chapter four, and other scripture. *"Submit yourselves therefore to God. Resist the devil, and he will flee from you. Draw nigh to God, and he will draw nigh to you"* (James 4:7-8). Ava prayed the words of scripture as God recalled them to her mind.

As she prayed aloud, she heard other students in her class confessing their sins and praying for Jesus to deliver them. She felt surrounded by an almost tangible presence of the Holy Spirit as she ministered to each of the children in turn.

"The Spirit of the Lord poured out His love on me in a new way. I realized that even though I had given my life to serve these people, I had not truly loved them until this momentous day when I was immersed in the love of Jesus. As I listened to their confessions, I was broken with love for them," Ava said.

The class period ended, but the time of prayer continued. The children were scheduled for her husband's history class, but instead, he came to the typing classroom. Others joined them, and a time of praise and worship continued for the rest of the day and into the night.

Soon after this mountaintop experience in 1963, Ava attended a Bible seminar presented by Dr. William Standish Reed, who, in addition to the practice of medicine, traveled around the country presenting Bible seminars.

"I received the gift of tongues at this seminar and shared the experience with no one," Ava said. "A while later in the same year, Albert also received the gift of tongues. And then we had such joy as we shared this privilege with each other."

Their mission board didn't believe the gift of tongues, described in the New Testament, was given after the close of the Apostolic age, and when they found out that the Steiners practiced this gift, they asked them to withdraw from the mission. The Steiners were no longer in agreement with the board's stated theological position.

"It was a devastating experience, for we had invested our lives in this mission and felt this intense love for the people. We had no choice but to leave, and in July 1963, the Lord led Albert to accept a call to pastor a Methodist church in Greensburg, Pennsylvania."

In October of their first year there, Albert read an ad in a Pittsburgh newspaper, announcing a series of meetings at St. Paul's Episcopal Church in Mount Lebanon, a community seven miles south of the city. They decided to attend the meetings, and they were inspired by the speakers and encouraged by the warm welcome. Almost forty years later, Ava recalled meeting two women at the conference whose friendship would change her life.

"I still remember the immediate sense of love Tibb Gethin and her friend Florence Holtz conveyed," Ava said, smiling as she remembered the circumstances of their meeting. "There was an intermission between seminars, and I pushed open the door of the lady's lounge, and there they were, sitting with their shoes off and their feet up. They invited me to join them, and I was glad to rest my feet for a little while, too.

"Before long, Tibb began to tell me about the spiritual happenings in Mount Lebanon. There was a radiance about her, a childlike quality of enthusiasm that few people retain as adults.

"At that time, Albert and I felt that we were living in a desert with no one to talk to about the wonderful experiences we had as missionaries in southern Texas. I was thrilled when I heard how God healed Dolly's heart and told Tibb to start a prayer group in her home."

Ava felt God's love in their presence and she was encouraged to tell them about the revival on the mission field and the way they were rejected when they began to use the gift of tongues in prayer. Ava was crying as she finished telling the story to Tibb and Florence, and they were crying with her.

"The Lord really melted us together that day. Tibb asked if I would come and tell my story at the Wednesday Morning Prayer Group, and soon after that, Albert and I decided to go," Ava said.

"We were received with open arms, and it was so wonderful to meet people who didn't question us about our theology. They just received us as fellow Christians. By the time we had attended a few meetings, we loved and trusted these precious Christians."

The hour-long drive between Greensburg and Mount Lebanon became their highway to healing from the inner wounds they had experienced when the mission asked them to leave.

"We received wonderful spiritual food every week. We were not only blessed as individuals but often received direction in our pastoral work."

Ava and Albert believe they were blessed through Tibb's ministry in order to be a blessing to others. They attended regularly for more than twenty years, sharing the love God continued to pour out through them.

"I believe that, aside from the important work of leading people into a personal relationship with Christ and her prayers for healing, Tibb was used mightily in a work of reconciliation within the Body of Christ," Ava said.

"Methodists Lutherans, Episcopalians, Presbyterians, Pentecostals, Catholics and Charismatics, as well as people of many races and nationalities, met with equality in her home. Through the ministry of the Holy Spirit, they were melded into a praying fellowship," Ava said.

As early as 1963 when the Steiners came to the group, Tibb knew of 300 prayer groups that had spun off through people who had attended the group.

"We were in the vanguard of a move of the Holy Spirit that was sweeping across the world," Ava said. "Those of us who attended the prayer group began to hear reports of God's work through people He led there from many places. Each week we looked forward to hearing from unexpected visitors to Tibb's home."

In addition to their ministry through the Wednesday Prayer Group, Albert served as a pastor in both Greensburg and Beaver County churches. Ava led a large prayer group in her New Brighton home until her death in 2003.

# Chapter 12
## Never, Never, Give in

> *But false prophets also arose among the people,*
> *just as there will also be false teachers among you,*
> *who will secretly introduce destructive heresies,*
> *even denying the Master who bought them, bringing*
> *swift destruction upon themselves* (2 Peter 2:1).

TIBB WELCOMED THE STEINERS INTO THE FELLOWship with joy and appreciation. Others who exercised the gift of tongues privately were also melded into the praying fellowship, but this gift was not practiced publicly in the weekly meetings.

"I didn't seek any of the gifts of the Holy Spirit," Tibb said. "I sought the Giver, and I was available and willing to serve Him in any way He directed me. When people asked me if I had the gift of tongues, I said, no, God never exercised that gift through me, not in all my years of ministry."

She turned the pages of her Bible to the twelfth chapter of I Corinthians, in order to identify some of the gifts she and others in the group were chosen to exercise.

"The scripture is clear," Tibb said. "As Christians, we are like various parts of a human body and we have different functions. He equips us for these functions."

Her love for God's Word was evident in the buoyant timber of her voice when she read a scripture to illustrate her point and the scripture was always her reference.

"Just listen to this," she said as she turned the worn pages of her Bible.

> *But to each one is given the manifestation of the Spirit for the common good. For to one is given the word of wisdom through the Spirit, and to another the word of knowledge according to the same Spirit; to another faith by the same Spirit, and to another gifts of healing by the one Spirit, and to another the effecting of miracles, and to another prophecy, and to another the distinguishing of spirits, to another various kinds of tongues, and to another the interpretation of tongues.*
>
> *But one and the same Spirit works all these things, distributing to each one individually just as He wills. For even as the body is one and yet has many members, and all the members of the body, though they are many, are one body, so also is Christ. For by one Spirit we were baptized into one body, whether, Jews or Greeks, whether slaves or free, and we were all made to drink of one Spirit* (1 Corinthians 12:7-13).

She seemed reluctant to tear herself away from the Word, and when she stopped reading, she commented that memories were flooding her mind—memories of ways in which God trained her to recognize His prompting to exercise these gifts.

"This isn't all of the gifts we receive from the Holy Spirit," Tibb said. "These are some of the more easily recognized gifts."

She had seen Kathryn Kuhlman exercise a gift of faith and knowledge when she called out that Dolly was being healed. Gifts of healing were at work as God restored Dolly's health. "This is a cluster of gifts that I saw God use over and over in the Wednesday Prayer Group," Tibb said.

She continued to describe other gifts that God taught her to use and understand. "The word *miracle* is used very loosely in our day and age. We use it to describe healing "miracles," but miracles in the Bible also include God's control over the natural elements. God parted the Red Sea so that the Israelites could escape the Egyptian army. Jesus calmed a raging storm and multiplied five loaves of bread and two fish to feed thousands of people.

"The gift of prophecy is often misunderstood as well," she continued. "The first thought that comes to your mind when you hear the word *prophecy* is somebody foretelling the future. Sometimes it may be future-telling, but more often a gift of prophecy is a word from the Bible that God wants to emphasize or call to someone's attention."

As she reflected on the gifts of the Holy Spirit and the way God taught her to exercise some of them, she recalled that learning about discernment and wisdom was the most painful lesson she had to learn.

"We always focus on the joy of serving the Lord and on the grace of answered prayer, but that isn't to say that we never experience the down side of life," Tibb said. "Learning to use the gift of distinguishing spirits, which is often called the gift of discernment, was painful for me.

"This is how God taught me. A woman came to the group, and for a short time she seemed to be sincere, but the woman's spoken prayers didn't ring true. She made me feel uncomfortable and these feelings were confirmed when she openly denied the deity of Christ and then others told me that she was trying to lead them into a cult," Tibb said.

Tibb and Dolly prayed privately about what God would have them do about the woman who was becoming more disruptive as the weeks went by. They decided they should ask everyone in the prayer group to attend a Kathryn Kuhlman meeting with them.

"I trusted Miss Kuhlman's spiritual counsel, and she had taken a special interest in our group," Tibb said. "You see, God, in His mysterious way, had told her that I would lead a prayer group through which He would work."

During the Kuhlman service that Tibb and the others attended, the evangelist, without prior knowledge of the situation, called the troublemaking woman out of the congregation and spoke to her. She told her not to go back to the prayer group.

The troublesome woman didn't go back to the Wednesday Prayer Group, but she began to harass Tibb. She called her on the phone at night. She knocked on her door at unexpected times, and when Tibb answered the door, she shouted accusations at her. "You're not a Christian or you would accept me and invite me back to the prayer group," was one of her most frequent accusations.

"It wasn't easy to be firm," Tibb said. "Because I was a Christian, I had given the Lord charge over my life. God was giving me direction, and I had to act upon it no matter how hard it was for me. I refused to allow her to come back to the prayer group."

Tibb's husband, Wynn, supported her whole-heartedly. He said, "Never, never give in." Peggy Hoffman, another member of the group, reminded Tibb how God taught her that some kinds of illness come forth only as a result of prayer and fasting. And wasn't this a type of illness? The group prayed and fasted, and soon the woman left them alone.

"God is stronger than the evil spirits that are in the world, and, through Christ, we have victory over them," Tibb said.

"We had to recognize Satan's activity, for at times when the group was growing or when major transitions were taking place, God allowed a troubling spirit to come among us," Tibb said. Sometimes the trouble was demonic, but more often it was a disagreement among some of the leadership about what the scripture meant, or a well-meaning person who would try to lead them away from the plan God had given Tibb for the group.

Through the book of Isaiah and other Old Testament books, God taught Tibb that the key to exercising His gift of discernment was to be faithful to study and obey His Word in the Bible.

"The Bible tells us that as we gain knowledge of His Word, we must also live a righteous life based on obedience to what we read. If I refuse to obey the Lord—which I have the free will to do—my disobedience clouds my ability to use God's gift of discernment. If I allow sin into my own life, how can God use me to help others escape Satan's power?

"As a nurse, I was trained to intellectually discern symptoms. This ability is based on the facts I have learned. As I submitted myself more and more to being a channel for God's Spirit, He began to use His gift of spiritual discernment through me. This gift allows us to recognize what is motivating a person or situation, and we must always act in love toward the troubled person," Tibb said.

She prayed that she would be obedient to God's Word, for she wanted the mind of Christ to be her preeminent guide. She studied the Gospels to learn what Jesus thought and how He acted.

"I discovered that His desire and delight were to be obedient to God, the Father. In the perfection of His sinless nature, Jesus understood God's will perfectly. Although we can never attain this perfection, I prayed to become as much like Jesus as I could be in this life," Tibb said.

# Chapter 13

## Where's the Prayer Meeting?

> *Opening his mouth, Peter said,
> "I most certainly understand now that
> God is not one to show partiality"*
> (Acts 10:34).

Pastor Archie Dennis was one of the Wednesday Prayer Group's favorite speakers, and he loved to tell about the first time he attended the meeting and how it changed his life. In the mid-sixties, he had a coveted position with one of Pittsburgh's major corporations. He was an African American who had cracked the glass ceiling to make a place for himself in a white man's world. Despite his success, he harbored some prejudice that wasn't pleasing to God.

"My grandma was a Pentecostal, and she enjoyed a lively worship service. She wasn't sure that the people in other churches were really saved. My mother and dad were Methodists. Between the two camps, I learned balance, but I also learned prejudice," Archie said.

"I remember when Sister Lucy Mae presented a prophetic word to me: she said I was the wrong color. She didn't mean that my color was wrong because my skin was black. She said that God needed to change the color of my heart."

He confessed that prejudice might have deprived him of fellowship within the larger body of Christ if he hadn't stumbled upon the Wednesday Morning Prayer Group.

"I was really searching and saying, 'God, there must be more than what I have been hearing,'" he said when he told his story at a prayer-group meeting. "I knew that God was up to something in my life, but I wasn't quite sure what it was. What would God want with me?"

Then one day he was at a public meeting and overheard two ladies talking about a prayer group. They were whispering, as though it were a secret.

"They weren't talking to me, but I butted in and said, 'Where is this prayer meeting?' They told me it was out in Mount Lebanon on McCully Street. I asked, 'When?' and they said it was every Wednesday morning at ten o'clock, but to get there early if I wanted a seat."

It took some courage to drive across town to a stranger's house. But he remembers that his hunger for the things of God led him there.

"I'll never forget the Wednesday morning that I first went. You see, coming from a Pentecostal background, I was used to women wearing high necks, long sleeves, long skirts, no makeup and no jewelry. Those were signs that our women were the "in group." We knew that women who didn't dress that way weren't going to make it to heaven. In fact, we weren't sure that anyone outside our church was going to heaven."

God put a crimp in Archie's thinking that Wednesday morning.

"I went to the house there in Mount Lebanon—on the

## Where's the Prayer Meeting?

other side of the tracks from where I lived. Mount Lebanon was the high-rent district even though the house was small; a duplex was not too much different from the other side of the tracks. When I rang the bell, a woman was standing there at the door and I couldn't deny the love of Jesus that showed upon her radiant countenance," Archie said.

"There was none of that 'know they are Christians by their dumpy clothes' either," he recalled. "She had on jewelry and makeup, like our folks said the women should not wear."

He sent up an instant message to the Lord. "God, you've got to help me."

"I went into that house, and there were about ninety more that looked like that lady at the door. Amen! Loving Jesus! I saw a beauty of holiness in them, and I could not deny the presence of Jesus as we just lifted our hands to Him and the love flowed.

"I saw miracles take place in that home. I saw sick bodies healed. People just sat in a blue chair and the ladies would lay their hands on them and minister in the Spirit. Across town, we said these folk weren't going to heaven, and suddenly I was like Peter in the Bible when the Lord told him that God was no respecter of persons," Archie said.

"It added a great dimension to my life to be freed of that prejudice against the folk on the other side of the tracks. That was more than twenty-five years ago, and I want everyone to know the profound influence Tibb Gethin has had on my life.

"She taught me that the Christian faith isn't in the outward appearance. It's in the love of God that is shed abroad in our hearts by the Holy Ghost. And now I no longer major on minors in the large multiracial church where I am a pastor. The same Jesus who saved you can tell you what to wear, and it isn't our business to take over His job of remodeling people.

"I praise God for what Tibb did for me and thousands of others," he concluded. "Rain or shine, she was there for hundreds of people every week. The devil tried to take her life, but God spoke one word and said, 'Live!,' and she was healed.

"Finally, the Wednesday morning group grew so large that she had to take it out of her house. I've seen more than one hundred people crowded there in her home on any given Wednesday, and now the prayer group meets in the Mount Lebanon United Methodist Church," Archie said.

"And it's awesome what God is still doing. Amen. Amen. Hallelujah! Forgive me; I just had to say that."

With the new awareness of God's love and impartiality in his heart, Archie was called to minister in music all over the world with the Billy Graham Crusade Ministry. When he retired after singing in more than eighty countries, God led him to pastor a large multiracial church in Monroeville, Pennsylvania.

When he spoke at the forty-fifth anniversary celebration of the prayer group in September 2000, five years after Tibb's death, he said that God was leading him to exhort all those who were there to make their bodies a living sacrifice to the Lord's service as Paul directed in his letter to the Romans:

> *I beseech you therefore, brethren, by the mercies of God, that ye present your bodies a living sacrifice, holy, acceptable unto God, which is your reasonable service* (Romans 12:1, KJV).

"I have only one life to give in worship. I want quality maximized," he said. "The King James Bible says this is a reasonable sacrifice, and I say 'Amen' to that, and then I think about how we can get started to obey the Lord's command.

"I think this way—God divides our years in the same way He divides the seasons of the year. From age one to twenty is the spring of our life; twenty to forty is summer; forty to sixty is fall; and from sixty to the end of our days is winter. He's designed every season of our lives as a praise offering to Himself, and we praise Him for it.

"Your praise and worship are the only two things you can give that He hasn't given to you. He's given us 168 hours in each week, and sixteen and one-half hours is the tithe of our time. If you spent as much time praying as you spend watching television, what would your prayer life be like?

"A tithe of your time is such a small offering when we compare it with our secular activities. When our life on Earth is ended, the opportunity to serve Him here will be gone. Whatever we would do for Him, we must do now.

"I say, tithe your time. It's a minimum expectation God has. All of us need improvement, and now is the time to become stewardly.

"Allow God to activate the talents and gifts He's given you to use, just as Tibb gave her life to God and was available as a channel for His love and power.

"*Be faithful until death, and I will give you the crown of life,*" the apostle John says in Revelation 2:10. This is God's word. He has placed you as salt and light in your neighborhood. The time will come when He will hold you accountable."

Archie closed his talk with a short but powerful prayer: "Father, thank you for the ministry of this prayer group for these prayer warriors who stand in the gap, interceding for those who need the touch of the Master. Amen."

## The House on McCully Street

(Pastor Archie Dennis was called home to heaven shortly after he presented this challenge to the hundreds of people who attended the prayer group's forty-fifth anniversary celebration.)

# Chapter 14
## Like a Mighty Wind

> *"And suddenly there came from heaven a noise like a violent, rushing wind, and it filled the whole house where they were sitting,"*(Acts 2:2).

WHEN THE HOLY SPIRIT SPOKE TO TIBB Gethin about starting a prayer group in her home, He told her that no two meetings would ever be the same. She could not have imagined in her wildest dreams the broad diversity of things God would do in answer to prayer.

Two meetings in particular illustrate different ways God accomplished healing, and they reminded Tibb of the first Pentecost when the Holy Spirit came upon the disciples after Jesus ascended into heaven. On a windless day, God sent a mighty wind blowing through the house, and on another Wednesday, His power descended upon an alcoholic to deliver him from his addiction.

On the day God sent the wind, Sarah and her husband, Claude, had driven in from Trafford (Dolly's home community north of Pittsburgh) to attend the meeting. Sarah had been coming regularly, but Claude had never been there before that day. Claude was embarrassed when he came in, and announced, pointing to his wife, "This woman brought me."

He was the victim of an accident at work that caused a piece of cement to lodge in his eye. He was unable to shed tears and refused to see a doctor, even though, try as he might, he couldn't get the cement out of his eye.

Early that Wednesday morning, Sarah had said to Claude, "Please, come to the prayer meeting with me today. The group will pray for your eye, and the cement will come out."

Claude came only because she insisted that the Lord could do it. When they came in, he sat next to his wife by the fireplace in Tibb's living room. When the meeting ended, people stood in little groups talking.

It was one of those hot, sticky days when there wasn't a breath of air outside and no sign that there would be for the rest of the day. All of a sudden, a strong wind swept through the dining room and the living room. Just a big sweep of wind. Everyone who was there felt it.

And as the wind swept through the living room, Claude started to cry out loud. Tears were streaming down his cheeks, and the piece of cement fell out of his eye instantly. Someone started to sing, and Claude thought he had died and gone to heaven—so he told the women later.

"This was a man who for years did all the carpentry and all the painting free of charge in the Trafford church," Tibb commented. "He did everything for the church, but never had a close relationship with Jesus. That day, Claude found the Lord in the wind at the prayer group."

Until he died in 1988, Claude repeated the story of the mighty wind God sent to heal his eye. He also told them about his spiritual experience—how Jesus became so real to him and the angels were singing all around him—and how he cried the whole time.

"You know, the Lord has never repeated an experience that we've had on Wednesday mornings," Tibb said. "We never have had that wind since then. He does those things to show us His power. And He is with us always.

"That wasn't the only time some of us saw or heard angels at the meeting. A couple of times, some of us saw angels in the church sanctuary after the group moved to that larger space," she said.

"I saw them one time on the left side of the sanctuary. In fact, they were all singing to the music. You just can't tell things like that to everyone, can you?"

She admits that the story of the anonymous alcoholic who came to the prayer group is pretty incredible, too, and for that reason, God acted when there were more than one hundred witnesses to confirm what He did.

Tibb didn't know the two women who brought the young man with a serious alcohol problem to the prayer group. The twenty-seven year old man was a resident at the Torrence Center for Alcohol Rehabilitation near Pittsburgh.

"At the time, the prayer group was growing so fast that we were everywhere in the house—up the stairs, down the hallway and into the kitchen," Tibb said. "The women brought him because they thought that God could help him. Bless these two women! To this day I don't know who they were, but the Lord does.

"Well, when they arrived, one of them whispered in my ear that the young man really needed prayer. They took him back to the dining room, which was quite full of people at that time. The meeting went on. Then, as we were concluding our morning together, I realized we had not had any audible prayer for that young man. Unbelievable.

"I kept saying in my heart, 'Lord, we haven't prayed for that young man.' Usually we sat a person in the blue chair in the living room for special prayer. Then we would gather around and those who were led of the Lord would pray. These were my plans for this young man, but the Holy Spirit chose another way to heal him of his alcoholism," Tibb said.

At the close of the meeting, the young man made a dash for the front door, as fast as he could move, stepping over and around the people. As Tibb opened the door for him, he fell backward under the power of God.

"He landed at my feet with such force that those coming down the stairway, directly across from the front door, fell backward against the steps. There he lay for quite some time as everyone sat quietly praying for him. Finally he got up, and his face was shining. Absolutely shining. He didn't say a word as he walked out the door. The two women who brought him followed him," Tibb said.

"No one knew his name or the name of the two women who had brought him, but many people saw the radiance of Christ shining on his face. He was like Moses coming down the mountain after his encounter with God.

"About two years later, I was at Russell Bixler's church in Squirrel Hill, on the other side of Pittsburgh," Tibb continued. "Would you believe that those two women who had brought the young man were there?

"They said, 'Tibb, have you ever heard anything about the young alcoholic man we brought to your prayer group?' I told them that I didn't know what had happened after he left my home."

The women told Tibb that on that day, when they drove him back to Torrance, he kept exclaiming about the beauty of the leaves on the trees and he was excited about every little flower he saw from the car window. He said it was the first time in years that he had seen them. The world was just beautiful to him, and he kept asking us to look and see how wonderful everything looked.

"They went on to tell me that he was released from the rehab center at Torrance shortly after he had been to the prayer meeting and he hasn't touched a drink since that day," Tibb said.

"They told me that he was married, has a family and a good job. God's work in him was complete in that one moment on a Wednesday morning.

"You see, this is why we've been told not to interrupt God's work, since the Holy Spirit has His own special way of working with each individual. Each time, it's different, and we never cease to be amazed at the new miracles of grace He allows us to observe.

"I'd like to meet that young man someday. Maybe he'll come back. I don't even know his name."

# Chapter 15

## Trapped in the Dining Room

> *For God has not given us a spirit of timidity, but of power and love and discipline* (2 Timothy 1:7).

MANY PEOPLE WERE HEALED OF MENTAL ILLness through the Wednesday Prayer Group. Tibb remembered the stories of two women in particular, because she knew them well and they continued to attend the group for many years after they were healed.

Doris doesn't remember who told her about the Wednesday Morning Prayer Group. She came alone and found the house, which was very crowded that morning. She does remember that she recognized the inside of the house as one she had seen in a dream a few nights before she came, and this gave her the courage to push her way through the living room despite her fear of cramped spaces.

It was the mid-sixties, and Doris had been under psychiatric care for eight years. Claustrophobia was only one of the symptoms that blighted her life.

"I did very strange things," Doris said. "I shook out my shoes each morning to make sure there were no spiders in them. I was afraid to get on an elevator or escalator, and I had an obsessive fear of going through tunnels. I was afraid to drive my car. I was afraid of everything. I came into the house because of the dream, but by the time I was in the middle of that house overflowing with people, it was too much for me to bear."

She went into panic mode and fled through the kitchen down the basement stairs, hoping there might be a way out, but she couldn't find the door. In a frenzy, she ran up the steps, through the kitchen and managed to get back to the archway between the dining room and the living room. By that time, it was almost ten o'clock and she found herself stranded there.

"No one knew me. No one knew the severity of my obsessions. No one seemed to notice my harried attempts to escape. There I was, poor soul, stuck between the two rooms and afraid to ask anyone to help me," Doris said.

"Suddenly, as I stood there, the power of the Lord came down and healed me completely. It was like the whole load of fears was lifted. When they asked for testimonies that morning, I told that group of strangers what had happened and that instead of fear, I was floating in peace. I was free."

When the meeting ended, Doris got in her car and drove through the Fort Pitt Tunnel to meet her husband in downtown Pittsburgh. She sang "What A Friend We Have In Jesus," all the way through the tunnel. She parked in front of the Hilton Hotel and waited for her husband to come out. He couldn't believe his eyes when he saw her parked there.

"Of course, I went back to the prayer group as often as I could, and the crowd never bothered me and none of my symptoms ever returned," Doris said. "Such a wonderful Lord we have and what a wonderful healer. He saved me before I knew enough to pray."

Doris has never had a recurrence of her disturbing mental condition, and in recent years, she is taking care of older women in her home.

Ruby Haff's friend, Winnie, also experienced an immediate healing after a suicide attempt. Doctors were amazed that she recovered and that she had no brain damage.
In a recent interview, Winnie recalled the events that led up to the day she ingested twenty-four sleeping pills that a doctor had prescribed for her mother.

"My father died at the age of forty-nine, and my mother was very dependent on me," Winnie said. "For twenty-five years, I was her caregiver, in addition to taking care of my husband and three children. My mother didn't live with us until 1970, but she was never satisfied with the apartments she rented, and we helped her move nineteen times."

Winnie's husband, Bob, worked for the International Division of a large Pittsburgh corporation, which meant that he was out of the country a lot of the time.

"When he was home, he was experiencing jet lag and he kept awake by drinking a lot of coffee," Winnie said. "He wasn't home enough to notice that I was depressed, and I didn't recognize the symptoms. It seemed that I was tired all the time, but that was to be expected with the heavy workload I was carrying, for the most part, on my own."

By the time her mother moved in with them in 1970, the couple's first two children were teenagers and they had a daughter who was three-and-a-half-years old.

"My mother didn't want me out of her sight," Winnie recalls. "I couldn't leave the house even to go to the store.

## The House on McCully Street

If we needed groceries or medication for her, our son, Tim, had to go for them on his bike. He wasn't old enough to drive at the time."

Her mother didn't sleep well, and the doctor prescribed a sleeping medication. The first night she gave her mother one of the pills, her mother slept until eleven o'clock the next morning and was like a zombie the rest of the day. Winnie called the doctor, and he called in a different prescription. He suggested that Winnie put the first pills away where their youngest child couldn't reach them. He believed her mother would need the stronger medicine later, as she had a terminal illness.

"I put the pills in the high cupboard over the stove and didn't give them any further thought," Winnie said. "Mother died on the day after Thanksgiving, and my grief was mixed with relief because I had a serious back problem and caring for her was very difficult."

Winnie was taking a lot of pain medication, and their son, Tim, was doing much of the housework. Their eldest daughter, Jenny, was in college at the time. Then, Tim broke his wrist and couldn't help.

"It was an extremely stressful time, but I didn't know I was depressed about the situation," Winnie said. "The weekend that I took the pills, Jenny was home for spring break and my husband, Bob, had come home for one of his usual weekends. As I mentioned, he drank a lot of coffee, and that morning I pulled the mug rack out—it was on a track in the cupboard over the stove.

"As the rack slid forward, the bottle of sleeping pills dropped into my hand. I had never had thoughts of suicide, but in that instant, the thought sprang into my mind that my family would be better off without me. I poured the

## Trapped in the Dining Room

coffee for Bob, kissed him and then walked into each of the children's rooms and kissed them."

Winnie went into the couple's bedroom and locked the door, something she had never done before. She went into the bathroom and swallowed twenty-four pills that were strong enough that her doctor said four would have killed her.

"As soon as I took the pills, I laid my clothes out and got in the shower. I wanted to be fresh and clean for the undertaker."

Her daughter, Jenny, wondered why her mother had kissed her that morning and when she asked the other children, they said she had kissed them, too. She tried her mother's bedroom door and found it locked, although she could hear the shower running. She rushed down to the kitchen and asked her dad if he had quarreled with her mother. He said, "No," but she had kissed him before she went upstairs. He, too, felt concerned about the locked door and they rushed upstairs.

"Bob kicked the door in and saw the pill bottle on the sink," Winnie said, continuing her story. "I was standing there, dressed as if I were ready to leave the house. He asked me if I had taken the pills. I told him I'd taken all of them. He knew how strong those pills were and immediately called the police and the paramedics."

Winnie felt the effects of the medication coming on fast, and the last thing she remembered was the Mount Lebanon policeman kneeling beside her with tears streaming down his face pleading with her to go to the hospital with them. He said he didn't want to take her by force. They couldn't lay her on a stretcher because she would have become unconscious faster.

"Bob told me that between them they got me into the police car, and when they got to the emergency room, they were holding me under the arms to carry me in. They said a thoracic surgeon was there and he cleared my airways, but when he heard what I'd taken, he didn't offer them much hope. They called our family doctor to confirm what medication I'd taken. They said I mumbled, 'I don't want to live,' before I went totally out," Winnie recalled.

She woke up forty-eight hours later and saw their pastor, Dr. Winston Trevor, standing beside the bed, praying for her. Ruby Haff was holding her hand.

"My daughter had called Ruby Haff, who was my neighbor before we moved," Winnie said. "We were close friends."

Ruby was overwhelmed with grief. She knew that Winnie had been looking for spiritual answers, but she didn't realize she was depressed. She called many of the women in the prayer group and asked them to pray for a miracle, and then she came to the hospital and stayed with Winnie.

"I was in the hospital for two weeks, and the Lord provided me with a 'born again' nurse. I remember how she shook me awake the first time and said, 'God has saved you and you're a miracle. No one could take all that medicine and live.'

"Despite a miserable headache and double vision, I was whole," Winnie said. "I told the nurse that I wanted to die and go to heaven, and when she discovered that I wasn't a Christian, she said, 'Don't you know that you would have gone to hell if you died?' I told her that no one goes to hell, because God is love. The nurse shared the scripture with me that showed that without Jesus, I would surely have gone to hell."

Everyone who attempts suicide must see a psychiatrist before leaving the hospital, and the psychiatrist talked to her about the subtleties of depression. She learned that the huge burden she had carried passively had been tearing her down emotionally. No one had recognized the problem, because she kept everything to herself.

"I went to counseling for a while, and Bob insisted on going, too," Winnie said. "Ruby and Tibb took me to a Kathryn Kuhlman meeting, and Miss Kuhlman called me up to the altar, and when she touched me, I went down. I got up and she touched me again, and I fell down again. She told me that I was falling under the power of God as He completed my healing."

Winnie accepted Christ that same day and continued to attend the prayer group that was meeting in the Methodist Church at that time.

"All of my family accepted Christ within a very short time," Winnie said. "The Lord blessed us with a miracle, and I can't put into words how grateful I am. My husband Bob credits the prayer group with my 'normalcy,' and I know he's right. Since his retirement, Bob attends the prayer group with me when he is able."

# Chapter 16
## *The Blue Chair*

> *"Praise Him with the timbrel and dancing;*
> *Praise Him with stringed instruments and pipe...*
> *Let everything that has breath praise the* LORD.
> *Praise the* LORD*!"* (Psalm 150: 4-6).

EVERYONE WHO CAME TO THE PRAYER GROUP wasn't healed, and it was a great disappointment to Jean Yocum that a young girl, who was afflicted with a serious mental illness, left without seeking help. Gretchen was in the high-school Sunday school class Jean taught at the Mount Lebanon United Presbyterian Church. The teenager was moody and her dress slovenly. She wasn't the kind of person Jean liked to be around.

Jean preferred to surround herself with attractive and talented people. She taught Sunday school and sang in the choir at the United Presbyterian Church, but she lived her real life at the country club where she enjoyed swimming and golf in the summer and rounds of parties with friends outside the church in the winter months.

For several years, the Lord had been speaking to Jean through Dr. Cary Weisiger, who was the pastor of her church. The Bible had been coming alive to her, and she was increasingly aware that Jesus had mingled with the sick, the poor and physically unattractive people. She wanted to run from Gretchen, but what she was learning about God kept drawing her back to the troubled teenager.

"When I told my friend Ruth Maxwell about Gretchen, she urged me to take her to the Wednesday Prayer Group she attended. She told me that she had seen people healed of mental illness. When I look back on this, I believe Ruth recognized that I needed some help myself," Jean said.

Jean knew a little about spiritual healing, and she didn't feel awkward about attending a prayer meeting.

"I kept watching Gretchen during the meeting, and she just sat there like she wasn't paying much attention to anything. I was disappointed that she left as soon as the meeting was over without even saying goodbye. I didn't plan to stay myself, but Dolly Graham came over to me and said, 'Jean, would you like some prayer?'"

"Oh, no," I said. "I'm fine, thank you. It was my friend who needs prayer, but she left."

Dolly said, "Well, you know more about your friend than the rest of us do. Why don't you sit in for her as an intercessor?"

Jean had never heard of anything like that in her life. She hesitated, and before she knew it, Dolly and others talked her into sitting in the blue chair, that special chair that was becoming a symbol of answered prayer.

"I sat down, and they began to pray for me," Jean recalls. "All of a sudden something hit me that was very different. I knew immediately that it was the power of the Holy Spirit through the intercessory prayer of these caring Christians. I saw the face of Jesus in the people there. I felt His presence and His healing touch through their laying on of hands in prayer. I felt like I was immersed in the love of God."

Jean got up from the blue chair and left the house right away. She had a date that afternoon to play bridge with some friends. They had to play three-handed bridge that day because she didn't keep her date. She didn't even call to explain her absence until that evening.

"I thought I was floating, just floating on a wave of God's power. And I truly was. That precious day at the prayer meeting took care of the way I'd been running away from sick and disfigured people. I knew that whatever had happened to me, I was like a new person, and I was gifted to love people I would have shunned in the past. I felt like one who had been dead and had come alive."

Jean called her mother and told her how wonderful Jesus was. Her mother was apprehensive about the experience.

"Please don't turn into a roly holer," her mother quipped, making a joke of the term "holy roller."

The next time her mother visited from out of state, she attended the prayer meeting and seemed to accept the group as something positive in Jean's life.

As in every aspect of the leadership of the prayer group, God spoke to Tibb and told her that He had gifted Jean to lead music in the group.

"I never liked the guitar," Jean said. "My father used to play guitar. Many evenings he would invite some men to our home to play Hawaiian guitars. They would sing hillbilly songs. I always thought that it was the worst music I'd ever heard in my life, and I never wanted any part of it. It was barnyard music to me.

"I loved the kind of high church music I sang at the Mount Lebanon U.P. Church. The minister of music used a lot of classical hymn tunes, and I enjoyed the quality of a big church choir—a wonderful pipe organ and great soloists. My voice isn't solo quality.

"Yet, I really felt that Jesus was calling me to make a joyful noise to the Lord. The whole idea of singing in a prayer group or using guitars in a church service hadn't been done before. Instead of singing songs from the hymnbook, the leader teaches the words and the people have to look at the leader to sing along. It keeps the group focused."

Tibb recalled that, as Jean stepped out on faith to do something alien to her own tastes, the Lord blessed her mightily. She was given the ability to respond to the Holy Spirit, moving from one chorus to the next seamlessly. She taught the words so easily that no one had trouble singing along.

Jean remembers some of the favorite choruses that the group loved to sing: "He Touched Me," "Oh, How I Love Jesus," "Rejoice in the Lord," "It is Well With My Soul," "Amazing Grace," "Blessed Assurance," and "My God Can Do Anything."

She also remembers her friendship with Ruby Haff, who shared the music ministry, and Ava Steiner, who introduced new songs to her repertoire. She recalls with appreciation many others who, as the size of the prayer group increased, were called by God to join her in leading the singing, which was a way of praising God.

"I was obedient to God's call, and through this group God brought me into a personal relationship with His Son that I'd never known before," Jean said. "I pray that the work He called me to has all been to His glory."

## Chapter 17
## *The Blind Receive Sight*

> *"The blind receive sight and the lame walk,
> the lepers are cleansed and the deaf hear..."*
> (Matthew 11:5a).

By 1965, Tibb recognized an ever-widening circle of relationships fanning out from the prayer group. The original members may have anguished over the indifference they encountered from friends they invited. They waited months for others to join their joyous fellowship. But within a few years, a multiplication factor kicked into play. They saw the group poised to become a large congregation of the faithful.

Needy people heard about answered prayer and flocked to Tibb's house, where they believed she could help them tap into God's power. "I can't do anything for you," she was often heard to say, "but I can introduce you to Jesus, the one who holds the keys to the Kingdom of God."

The surging tide was well underway when Jean Yocum brought her guitar to the meeting. Her exuberant music drained away the tension of heartaches, trouble and fear. People responded to her charismatic personality, and, if her father had lived to hear her play, he might have recognized elements of that country hoedown sound that she had hated in her youth.

Jean began to invite her friends to come to the meeting, and Bert Thomas was the first one she told about the group that meant so much in her life. Jean was surprised that Bert didn't come immediately, because she knew Bert believed in praying for the sick. Her husband, Bud, had lost his hearing in one ear due to a diving accident, and his hearing had been miraculously restored through the ministry of Kathryn Kuhlman.

"I thought I was too busy to go to the prayer group," Bert recalls. "But the time came when I couldn't put off going, because Bud's friend, Lou, who had a back problem, wanted us to take him to Tibb's prayer group."

Lou was in great pain one day when Bert and Bud were visiting him. He was in so much pain that he was miserable, and doctors hadn't found any relief for him. In order to encourage Lou to believe that God could heal his back, Bud told him the way God had instantly healed his ear to the amazement of his doctors.

Bud offered to take Lou to a Kathryn Kuhlman meeting. Lou was a devout Catholic and didn't want to go. Bert told him about the prayer meeting in a home in Mount Lebanon where people also received healing through prayer. Bert told him that she'd never been there but had been invited and would be glad to go with him. Lou said he'd think about it.

Not long after that, Lou called Bert to say that the pain had become more severe and he couldn't stand it. He said he didn't want to go back into the hospital and he hoped that Bert would take him to the prayer group.

"The day we went, it was truly wall-to-wall people and

## The Blind Receive Sight

we couldn't find a seat," Bert said. "Bess Rasp, who was one of Tibb's helpers, found us a place to sit," Bert said.

"After the meeting, I suggested that Lou go into the dining room for special prayer. Ruby Haff and Dorothy Collins were the only two people I knew who were there at the time. They prayed for Lou. When he stood up, he was absolutely free from pain in his back. To date, Lou has had no pain whatever. What a praise to our good and merciful Lord!"

Bert became a regular at the Wednesday Prayer Group, and as she saw others healed, she thought about her sister who had been troubled by a rash all over her body for several months.

"My sister lived in North Carolina, and one night she called to say that the rash was so bad that she had to spend four hours each day in the tub filled with medicated water in order to get some relief from the pain," Bert said.

"I told her that the next time I went to the prayer group, I would ask them to pray for her. She told me later that at the time the group was praying for her, she was sitting at her kitchen table and felt like something was touching the top of her head. A current seemed to pass clear through her, and within two to three days, the rash was completely gone." Bert and Bud had only begun to witness the power of God through their testimony. Bert continued her story:

"Bud is an attorney, and one day, Dick, who is also an attorney, told him that he couldn't see out of one of his eyes. Bud drove the young man to the downtown office of the company's physician. The doctor diagnosed an unusual eye disease and sent him to the 'eye and ear hospital' for further tests," Bert said.

"From this Pittsburgh Hospital, Dick went to hospitals in Ohio and Maryland, where he was told the disease could spread and he could lose the sight in the other eye. Doctors in both hospitals recommended that the sight in the bad eye be completely destroyed to prevent the disease from spreading to the good eye.

"I told Bud that I would take the problem to the prayer group so they could pray about it. The day after we prayed, Bud asked Dick how his eye was, and Dick said that the day before had been the best day he'd had in several months.

"Bud told Dick that the prayer group had prayed for him the previous day. Dick said to tell them to keep praying. The next week, they prayed again, and the disease in Dick's eye completely disappeared. And Dick, who wasn't a Christian, didn't even go to the prayer group, yet he was healed," Bert said.

Dick returned to the Maryland hospital, and the doctors were amazed that his eye was perfectly normal. Dick told Bud what the doctors said and he asked Bud to have Bert thank the prayer group. He was very grateful that people cared enough to pray.

"Why not go and thank them yourself?" Bud suggested.

After some hesitation, Dick agreed to go and thank the prayer group. The morning that Dick went to Tibb's, he heard the gospel presented and gave his life to Jesus Christ, and his life was changed.

"I'd say that spiritual healing was as great a miracle as the physical one," Bert concluded.

Shortly after that, Dick moved to Ohio where he joined the Episcopal Church and became an active leader. Later, he joined a Christian law firm in Washington D.C. and continues to witness to his faith in Jesus. The prayer group con-

## The Blind Receive Sight

tinued to pray for Dick, and as the years passed, they praised God for the work of the Holy Spirit that flowed through him to many others.

## Chapter 18
### Waiting for God's Will

> *"Take my yoke upon you, and learn of me;*
> *for I am meek and lowly in heart: and ye shall find rest*
> *unto your souls. For my yoke is easy and my burden*
> *is light"* (Matthew 11:29-30, KJV).

TIBB RECALLED THAT, EVEN AFTER THE PRAYER group moved from the house on McCully Street into the sanctuary of the Mount Lebanon Methodist Church, she could not walk into her living room without feeling the presence of God and His glory that was so powerful during the seventeen years the group met in her home.

"We kept boxes of tissues handy," she said. "It was as if the Holy Spirit came in, and we didn't always know whether He was pushing out the sadness to make room for His joyful presence or if the tears were simply an overflowing of joy."

She remembered the morning Sally Fahringer brought her friend Maggie to the prayer group for the first time. They were especially touched by the music led by Jean Yocum, and they reached for the tissue more than once as their tears flowed through most of the two-hour meeting.

"Their needs were met," Tibb said. "God gave them faith to love and patiently wait for God's will to be accomplished in the lives of family members. It was years before they would see their prayers answered, but they learned to wait upon the Lord."

Tibb remembered her dear friend Blanche Breslow who attended faithfully and always prayed that her Jewish husband would receive the Lord.

"All his life, he was faithful to the God of Abraham, and eight years before his death, the Holy Spirit touched his heart and he fell in love with Jesus. It was wonderful news for all of us who had prayed for him," Tibb said. "Blanche never pressured him. She simply lived an obedient Christ-like life, and I'd say that she loved her husband into the Kingdom."

Blanche brought her friend Betty to the prayer group and Betty told Tibb that from the first day she came, she experienced an insatiable desire to read the Bible daily, to pray, and to soak up everything at the meetings.

About the time Betty began to come to the prayer group, she was hearing rumors in the community that her husband was going to be released from his responsibility as head football coach at a local high school. He loved football, and it was his choice for a lifetime career. Yet, despite many winning seasons, he was fired. Betty was overcome with the sense of unfairness, and Tibb told her she needed to pray for the whole school board. Betty was shocked, and her reaction to what Tibb said wasn't unexpected.

"You must be kidding," Betty said to Tibb. "I can't pray for them."

"I understood the personal struggle she had with praying for people she felt had wronged her," Tibb said. "It wasn't the right time to remind her that Jesus was totally

## Waiting for God's Will

innocent when sinful men sent Him to the cross to die. I simply told her I would pray for the school board."

"I can do that for you," Tibb said to Betty.

"Not long afterward, Betty told me that she and her husband, Dan, felt the strength of the Lord when they faced the school board at various meetings and functions. You know the Holy Spirit is called the *paraclete* in the Greek language. He's the one who puts steel in our spine," Tibb said.

Dan wasn't restored to his position as football coach, but much to Betty's amazement, he was promoted to the position of Athletic Director for the high school, and he even got a raise. Through the power of prayer, their bitterness was washed away so that the Lord could act on their behalf.

"God just took that burden, and He will do the same for anyone who trusts Him. And oh, how Betty and Dan grew spiritually," Tibb said.

"I know Betty told Dan about the wonderful things the Lord did through the prayers of His believing people, and when he retired, Dan joined her in coming to the Wednesday morning meetings."

Tibb rejoiced with those whose prayers were answered immediately, and she rejoiced with those who allowed the Lord to walk alongside of them as they shouldered heavy burdens. Her friend Herta Kalbercamp was one of these people.

"Herta had been attending the group for some time, and I knew she was visiting a young man who was handicapped in many ways following an automobile accident," Tibb said.

"Sometimes Herta would ask to sit in the blue chair, the one where people often sat for special prayer. She was very concerned for this man and his family and felt frustrated that, despite prayer, there didn't seem to be any change in their situation.

"But, as time went on, I felt a growing knowledge in my spirit that Herta needed the Savior. She was working so hard to be like Jesus, but she didn't have the power of His Spirit to accomplish her goals. We just can't be all that He wants us to be until we surrender our lives to Him.

"On a particular day, the Holy Spirit touched Herta with power. She told me that He spoke to her in such a real way that she was moved to tears. Now Herta is the kind of person who doesn't like to show her emotions, and the next thing I knew, she was trying to get to the front door. She would have run out the door if she could have, but so many people blocked the way that it slowed her down. I was able to get to her before she got off the porch.

"I brought her back in and took her into the powder room, which is right behind the front door. And do you know, we hardly got in that tiny room before she accepted Jesus Christ as her Lord and Savior. Being present at the birthing of a babe in Christ is the most exciting experience in the Christian life, and we never can tell when God has that blessing in store for us—or where we'll be when the blessing comes!"

## Chapter 19
### The Roots of Cornerstone TeleVision

> *"Wives be subject to your own husbands, as to the Lord. For the husband is the head of the wife, as Christ also is the head of the church..."* (Ephesians 5:22-23).

THERE WAS NO GUEST REGISTER AT TIBB'S HOUSE. In all humility, she never kept a record of those who came to the group and received Christ, those who were healed or those who were empowered by the Holy Spirit to accomplish extraordinary tasks. The ministry God had in mind for Norma and Russell Bixler was one of the most unusual and one that demanded the continuing prayer support of the prayer group.

"Norma Bixler was sitting on the third step of the stairway in my living room when she accepted Christ," Tibb said. "I never cease to praise God for Norma's changed life and the ministry of Channel 40, Pittsburgh's Christian television channel, the ministry God called them to develop."

Norma was very angry with God when she came to the prayer group the first time. On that particular day, she was angry with her husband because he insisted that she go with him to the group. She was even more angry that he had become a minister when she had never planned to be a minister's wife.

"God called her husband into the ministry after they were married," Tibb said. "The Lord called him away from his proposed career as a lawyer and Norma's vision of herself as the wife of a successful businessman. Russell wrote about this in his first book, *It Can Happen To Anyone*," Tibb said.

Soon after Russell Bixler became the pastor of the Pittsburgh Church of the Brethren, an odd set of circumstances led the couple to come to the Wednesday Prayer Group. All kinds of ministries were springing up in the Pittsburgh Church of the Brethren, and one of them was a ministry to the families of people who came to Pittsburgh hospitals from out of town. The church provided housing and spiritual support for these family members while their loved ones were in the hospital.

A few days after Christmas in 1966, the Bixlers received an urgent call from a distant pastor asking for housing for the wife of a young man named Bill who had been struck by a car driven by a drunk driver. Bill had pulled his car onto the shoulder of the road to change a tire and his legs were crushed between the two cars. His kidneys were also damaged and failing from shock. One of the Pittsburgh hospitals possessed the only operative kidney machine within hundreds of miles.

Russell called Tibb on a Tuesday evening, asking her to pray for Bill. He hadn't met Tibb, but he heard that a prayer group met in her home on Wednesday mornings. He told Tibb that he felt it was urgent that he ask many people to pray or the man would surely die. She suggested that he come and bring the request himself.

## The Roots of Cornerstone TeleVision

"Russ and Norma came to intercede for someone else, but the Lord had brought them to the prayer group to work a miracle of healing in their marriage," Tibb said.

"Things weren't going too well between them, because Russ was pursuing the call of God on his life and Norma felt left out. She had never accepted Christ as her personal Savior, and I'm not sure Russ fully understood how frightened she felt by his call to serve God," Tibb said.

"Russell took seriously what he read in the book of Ephesians about wives being subject to husbands. He ignored the fact that Norma was a very independent person and she didn't think she needed to accept direction for her life from the Bible or from her husband."

Tibb remembered that one of the three things God had called her to do was to help bring harmony into marriage relationships. At the time, she didn't realize how important harmony between Russell and Norma would be for the Body of Christ at large.

"God had a plan to use them as an example of what He can do when one couple give their lives to Him and to each other," Tibb said. "The victim of the accident was healed over a period of several months, and that was obviously a miracle. What wasn't as obvious at first was that God was working a miracle of healing in their relationship."

Norma told Tibb that she didn't want to come to the prayer group that first Wednesday morning and that she and Russ had argued about it before they came. Norma only came after he laid the threat on her that Bill—the accident victim—would die if they didn't go to the prayer group but he wouldn't go without her.

"We look back and we know that Russ wasn't being fair to Norma, and we also know that she hadn't been honest with him. She hadn't told him how very angry she was with God and with him that her plans for her life were scuttled," Tibb said.

Norma's eyes looked a little red when she walked in the door of Tibb's house that first morning, and Tibb recognized how awkward Russell felt when he looked around the room and saw more than sixty women crowded into the small house.

"I know the signs," Tibb said. "Russ wanted to come, but when he got here, he wanted to turn around and run out. I also saw the tension in Norma relax, and she told me later that despite the fact that she didn't want to come, she felt enveloped in love from the minute she came through the door."

The group prayed for the accident victim at the beginning of the meeting. Russell had never attended a prayer meeting where he felt the presence of God as he did in Tibb's home. He knew that morning that, although he preached and prayed, he wasn't always a channel for God's love. Tibb talked about being filled with the Spirit, and he felt that he was missing something

The following Wednesday, Norma was the one who suggested they go back to the prayer group and Russell dragged his feet. Norma had done a turnaround, and wanted to find out more about how she could be like Tibb. She persuaded him to go back to the prayer group. Again, the prayer group prayed for the accident victim. His condition changed from week to week, and the Bixlers continued to come to the prayer group to intercede for him. Each week, the group also prayed for Russell and Norma.

The fifth Wednesday the Bixlers came to the prayer group, they went to lunch with Ruby Haff after the

## The Roots of Cornerstone TeleVision

meeting. Russell told Ruby about the tension between himself and Norma over spiritual matters, and Norma passively acknowledged what he said. She didn't tell either one of them that she had quietly prayed the sinner's prayer at Tibb's and accepted Christ as her Savior that morning. She didn't know what this would mean in her life, and she didn't know how to tell them.

"Russ asked if Norma could spend the afternoon with Ruby and me while he went back to work," Tibb said.

Alone with the two women, Norma confessed her new faith.

"Oh, what an afternoon of celebration we had. Hearing a new Christian's first confession of faith isn't unlike the feelings we have when we see the birth of a baby," Tibb said.

Russell picked Norma up and they drove home in silence. When they got home, she began to cry and Russell immediately knew that these were tears of joy.

"Russ told Norma that she had been washed clean by the blood of the Lamb," Tibb said. "She had always been a good wife and mother, but the couple had not been walking together with the Lord. God gave them a whole new relationship with each other and with Him.

"Shortly after Norma decided to follow Jesus, she told me that God had given her a vision of Christian television in Pittsburgh and she believed she and her husband should spearhead this project. The idea looked so impossible that the Wednesday group began to pray immediately," Tibb said.

Over the next ten years, the Bixlers were leaders in developing the Christian television channel that is currently Channel 40 in Pittsburgh. Until his death in 2000, Russell was Chief Executive Officer and Chairman of the Board and CEO of Cornerstone TeleVision. (The capitol "V" refers to the vision of God that motivated them and the power of God that brought the television channel into being.) Russell Bixler's book, *Faith Works*, published a few months before his death, tells how the Bixlers were God's agents in the development of the channel. Norma is continuing in the ministry.

In September 2000, when the prayer group celebrated its forty-fifth anniversary, Norma recalled the events surrounding her first visit to the prayer group.

"I didn't want to come to the prayer group," Norma said. "I had many excuses. When I got here I felt swallowed by love. Then I had a problem. I never had opened my heart to God. I was uncomfortable, and Tibb said, 'If Jesus is knocking on your heart's door, open the door. Will you open the door?'

"Jesus spoke to me and said, 'I've been waiting a long time.' I was sitting on the third step in her home when I said 'Yes,' and almost immediately Maxine George asked me what happened and I said to her, 'What do you mean when you ask what happened?'

"She said, 'I saw a light come into your eyes and I knew something wonderful happened. Tell me about it.'

"I'm so thankful for her asking that question so that Satan couldn't tempt me to doubt my commitment. I'm also thankful that both Russell and I discovered that the Power depicted in the Book of the Acts is with us still. It was through the prayer group that we began to walk together along a new and happier path.

"We took many needy people to the prayer group who subsequently watched Jesus miraculously turn their lives around. It was there that Russ and I received our first taste of life in the Spirit—the joy, the thrills, the excitement, the love, the power, the growth; in short, the Answer—Jesus Christ in the strength of His Holy Spirit.

"It was through Tibb that Russell received a prophesy about his ministry through Channel 40. One day she put her hand on his shoulder and quoted Isaiah as God's call on his life, and that scripture became Channel 40's guiding principle:

> *The Spirit of the Lord God is upon me, Because the Lord has anointed me To bring good news to the afflicted; He has sent me to bind up the brokenhearted, To proclaim liberty to captives, And freedom to prisoners* (Isaiah 61:1).

"No other words could more clearly state Tibb's mission in life and the mission she enlisted everyone in the prayer group to act out in their lives," Norma said.

"The Greater Pittsburgh community is a far better place to live because of Tibb Gethin. Only heaven will reveal all that God has accomplished in the many years the Holy Spirit has been active through the Wednesday Prayer Group."

# Chapter 20
## A Gift of New Songs

> "You are My witnesses,' declares the LORD,
> 'And My servant whom I have chosen...'"
> (Isaiah 43:10a).

Ruby Haff brought her friend Carol Nomides to the prayer group in the mid-sixties. Tibb often said that Carol was a blessing God sent into their midst at a time when people in the group were grieving the loss of a president and striving to cope with the growing tensions over Russians in Cuba and rebellion on college campuses.

Carol's stability was a comfort to Tibb and others. Like Tibb, she was a nurse, and Tibb always felt a strong affinity to people in the medical profession.

Carol had made a child's commitment to Christ, and she had served Him in a nominal way throughout her high school years. The church to her was a place where Christians gathered to listen to a sermon and sing a few hymns.

Her church was strongly committed to sending missionaries to foreign lands where "the heathen" needed to hear about salvation through God's Son, Jesus. It was a church

### The House on McCully Street

where she learned that those who attended other churches likely weren't Christians, and Catholics especially couldn't be Christians, because they believed a lot of things that weren't in the Bible.

Following high-school graduation in May 1949, Carol went into nurse's training, and in 1950, a friend invited her to go to a Kathryn Kuhlman service. These meetings were attracting a lot of attention because people claimed that they were supernaturally healed through prayer when Miss Kuhlman prayed for them.

"We were eighteen years old, and our motives weren't pure," Carol said. "We went out of curiosity, and I was ready to make fun of this woman with her flowing sleeves and that bony finger that she pointed around the congregation," Carol said.

"She preached a sermon that wasn't much different than the ones I'd heard throughout my childhood, except for the dramatic emphasis she added when she told Bible stories. When she preached the message of salvation, it tugged at my heart even though I knew I was a Christian. What Miss Kuhlman called 'ministry' followed the sermon.

"She would call out that various people were being healed by the power of God, and at first all I could see was that wagging finger. Then as I watched, she called out that somebody back in the area where I was sitting was being healed of a goiter.

"I looked around and then I saw this woman with the goiter, and as I watched, I saw the goiter shrink. 'Oh, my God,' I was saying to myself. 'My God.' It was very dramatic, and looking back I can see that God was preparing me for something, but at the time, I was just an observer. I did begin to read the Bible more seriously after I saw the woman healed."

Also, like Tibb, as Carol completed her nurses' training, her thinking was more focused on the science of nursing and the practice of nursing than on spiritual healing. She fell in love with Charlie Nomides, and their marriage was a happy one. They had three children by the time they moved to Dormont in 1962. Almost immediately, they joined a small Baptist church within walking distance of their home, and that's where Carol met Ruby.

"Charlie and I were both Christians, and we were bringing our three children up as Christians in ways that were similar to the way we grew up. I was looking for a fellowship of Christian women, so I didn't hesitate to go with Ruby to the Wednesday Prayer Group," Carol said.

She was impressed by the love that seemed to flow among the members, but she wasn't prepared for the ministry of prayer and healing.

"I knew Ruby was a leader in the group, and I may have even heard that God answered prayer for healing there, but it's a little different when you actually see your friend praying for someone and they fall flat on the floor. I ran over to the person and started to do my "nursey" thing, and Ruby said, 'It's okay. It's the Holy Spirit. God is intervening with power and that power has knocked her to the floor.'"

Carol had never seen anything like this. Years before, when she saw the woman healed of a goiter at the Kathryn Kuhlman service, she hadn't seen anyone fall on the floor, and she didn't know that Miss Kuhlman was exercising God's gift of knowledge in identifying a person God intended to heal. Ruby explained the gift of knowledge and told Carol that God sometimes used this gift through her so that she would know how to pray.

"Kathryn Kuhlman wasn't part of my life like Ruby. You can't really reject something that a friend tells you, especially if you see it happening," Carol said.

Ruby asked Carol if she was a Christian, and Carol said yes. Then, Ruby asked her if she would like to go with her to Russell Bixler's Sunday night prayer meeting.

"I had some uncertainty about all of this, but I wanted the power to live the kind of Spirit-filled life I saw in Ruby and Tibb. I decided to go, and at this meeting, I learned that God's power was available to Christians. I asked someone to pray for me that the Lord would baptize me in His Holy Spirit," Carol said.

"I was immediately aware of an intensified love for people and a desire that they, too, would come to a saving knowledge of Jesus Christ. In the days that followed, I noticed that I had a greater appreciation for all of creation and a spirit of gratitude that God had created such a world for me to enjoy. I still didn't understand much about this kind of ministry, and I began to study the book of Acts and other scripture."

Carol had the experience of speaking in tongues at the time she was baptized in the Holy Spirit at the church service led by Russell Bixler. Carol read in the Bible that sometimes this gift accompanied this Spirit-baptism and that the gift is an asset in intercessory prayer.

"Tongues is a way to let the Holy Spirit perfect my own prayer requests and praise—to bring them into line with God's will," Carol said.

She confided in Ruby that it was hard for her to accept the experience she had at Russell's Sunday evening prayer group. Ruby said she would grow into greater understanding and acceptance as she yielded her life more com-

## A Gift of New Songs

pletely to the service of God. Ruby encouraged her to participate in the leadership of the Wednesday prayer meeting and almost immediately asked her to sing.

"It was 1966 when this happened, and I soon realized that God had given me a gift of songs. Ruby knew this, and before very long, she began to ask me to sing for the group frequently and to teach them some of the songs God was giving to me.

"At first, I was petrified, but as soon as I began to sing, my fear vanished. I never knew when Tibb would say 'Sing Down at the Cross,' one of the songs I'd written that was her favorite."

Carol paused in telling her story to comment on what an unlikely person she was to be composing songs, singing solos and becoming a leader in the group.

"Tibb and God had more confidence in me than I had in myself. In high school, I had a severe lisp. I was determined to get over my fear of speaking. I'm a determined person, and I joined forensics and worked to overcome my fear of speaking. Eventually, I won the district and the regional competitions, but singing was a new step of faith. That's how God works—one step at a time. I tell you this to show you how shy I was," Carol said.

Carol was devastated when Ruby died in 1976. Ruby was her mentor and friend. God had healed Ruby of crippling arthritis. Why didn't He heal her of cancer?

"I thought to myself, 'How can I ever pray for healing for anyone again?' God's answer was to speak to me about His times and seasons and that to each human being there is a time to die. He spoke to me about His plan for me to take up Ruby's role as Tibb's assistant. I said to God: 'if that's the case, you'll have to tell Tibb,'" Carol said.

*The House on McCully Street*

The next Wednesday, Tibb came running down the aisle of the church and said, "The Lord woke me up and told me that Carol is to be my new assistant." That was the assurance Carol needed.

# Chapter 21
## Not Easy, But Victorious

> *"Husbands, love your wives, just as Christ also loved the church and gave Himself up for her"* (Ephesians 5:25).

TIBB'S DEAR FRIEND MARGARET WARNER ORIGInally came to the prayer group with her pastor's wife, Edna Lamont. Margaret and her husband, John, were active members of the First Presbyterian Church of Pittsburgh. They were committed Christians, leaders in congregational work.

Edna attended the prayer group regularly and often invited Margaret, but it wasn't until Margaret had a serious problem that she agreed to go. Her courage failed her when she tried to talk to anyone at the church about her personal life, and she thought perhaps she could talk to Tibb, who was a stranger.

The Warner's twenty-two-year-old daughter was pregnant out of wedlock.

"This was something that really hurt my pride. I was at my wit's end," Margaret recalled years later. "As I think back now, I was naturally concerned about our daughter. But I was more concerned for John and myself. Wild thoughts were running through my head—wondering if we had been good parents. How could this have happened to us?"

Margaret had looked forward to meeting Tibb, but when they got to the meeting, Tibb wasn't there.

"Ruby Haff and Ava Steiner were there, and so was Jesus," Margaret said. "As the meeting ended, Edna said to me, 'Why don't you ask Ava to pray with you?'"

I knew in my heart that the time had come for serious prayer. Ava asked me what I needed prayer for. I surely didn't want to go into my life history, and so I told her that I just needed prayer.

"Ava must have sensed in her spirit that I needed deliverance. She talked to me about it, but I told her that I had never heard the word *deliverance* and that I didn't know what she meant. She explained that Christians can be troubled by evil spirits that can take away their joy.

"I agreed that I was troubled, and if she thought I needed this kind of prayer then I was ready for it. She prayed in Jesus' name that I would be set free from any troubling spirit, and I felt the weight of pride and worry lifted from me. I had never felt such peace. My circumstances hadn't changed, but the Holy Spirit had come into my life in a new way," Margaret said.

Margaret's new security in Christ led her to attend the Charismatic Conference at Duquesne University to learn more about the work of the Holy Spirit. Many of her friends were going, and now she was ready to go with them.

Her husband, John, had serious back problems at that time and was recovering at home after back surgery. Since he was off work, he wanted to go with Margaret to the conference. She didn't want him to go.

"I'm ashamed to admit this, but I didn't want him to invade my own private time and my fellowship with Christian friends. The Wednesday Prayer Group was my escape so that I could get away without John. He probably wanted to go since he was alone so much of the time and, although he was a Christian, I shut him out of that part of my life," Margaret said.

She recognized later that her natural reserve was intensified when it came to her spiritual life. As a small child, she was blessed with an aunt who would read the Bible aloud before she went to sleep at night.

"I just loved our time together, and through her, I learned to trust Jesus and look to the Bible for direction for my life. I needed that support through the difficult years of my childhood," Margaret said.

As an adult, Margaret attended many Kathryn Kuhlman meetings where her faith was strengthened and she received healing through the Kuhlman ministry.

"I didn't tell anybody when I was healed at a Katherine Kuhlman meeting. It was something that I needed to keep personal for a while. In the same way, I was afraid that if I shared my personal commitment to Jesus with anyone else, they might reject my testimony and I wouldn't be able to handle the blow," Margaret confessed.

She knew that her husband had accepted Christ as his Savior at a church retreat and yet she continued to hide her own Christian experience from him.

"I was a reserved person, and when John received Jesus, he was far from reserved. Right away he began to go around telling everyone about his faith, and I was offended and embarrassed. I was very upset that he was such a fanatic, and I didn't support him in this at all."

She looks back at those years with tears: "I made a wonderful Pharisee at that time. I had all kinds of rules to live by. You don't do this and you don't do that. I was surely short on love for John, who was such a wonderful, spontaneous person. I really gave him a terrible time during that period of our lives, but eventually, through our relationship with Jesus and the way He sent Tibb and her husband, Wynn, into our lives, we resolved our differences and were happier than we had ever been."

She believes that the "deliverance" that began when Ava prayed for her became an ongoing work of the Holy Spirit far below the surface of her spiritual veneer. She harbored many bad attitudes that God began to heal through the prayer group and through the Charismatic Conference.

She became more open in her expression of her faith, especially to her husband. The time came when he went to the prayer group with her and immediately felt the warmth of the Holy Spirit extended to him through others in the group. He began to help Tibb's husband Wynn, who had also retired and was attending every week.

"John and Wynn had such wonderful rapport with each other and their sense of humor behind the scenes added a new dimension for all of those who helped with leadership. John had such a wonderful sense of humor," Margaret said.

For example, although Tibb was a humble person and never wanted anyone to put her on a pedestal, she did want to look nice. So the men would find ways to tease her. Tibb's husband would say to John, "Go tell Tibb her hair doesn't look good. If anything upsets her, it's when her hair isn't right."

John would go up to the front before the meeting and pass Wynn's message on to Tibb, who would thank him and rush off to check her hairdo. After awhile she caught on to them, but they were always thinking of new ways to make people laugh.

"How grateful I am that I had these years in which the four of us were friends in a shared ministry, for John and Wynn died within a few years of each other," Margaret said. "Tibb told me that John phoned her from the hospital the night before he died. He told her that he felt so good that he would be at prayer group the next Wednesday. He said, 'Tibb, I want to tell you that I found something at the prayer group that changed my life. Whatever you're doing, keep on doing it. I want you to promise me you'll keep on doing it.' Then he said 'Goodbye' to Tibb.

"John went to be with Jesus the next morning. How wonderful that God gave him time to say his goodbyes."

# Chapter 22
## A Healing Touch

> *These all with one mind were continually devoting themselves to prayer, along with the women...* (Acts 1:14a).

EVELYN WESTIN CAME TO THE PRAYER GROUP after she had an unusual experience following a cancer operation. The morning after the operation, she woke up in the hospital to the sound of wonderful music.

"It was heavenly music, and Jesus came into my room and touched me. He was surrounded by a great light, and I felt the realness of His hands and within my spirit I heard Him tell me not to talk about this experience," Evelyn said.

She wondered how she could learn more about what had happened to her if she didn't talk to anyone about it. Soon after that, her friend Ruth Robinson, who attended the Mount Lebanon Methodist Church, told her about the Wednesday Prayer Group and invited her to go. Another appearance of Jesus awaited her at the door of Tibb's house.

"As I walked up the steps onto the porch, I saw Tibb standing at the front door, and she was radiant and Ruby

## The House on McCully Street

beside her looking so beautiful, too. But it was the presence of the Lord that drew me into the group, because I saw Jesus standing between them, welcoming me. Tibb didn't need to tell me that the group belonged to Jesus," Evelyn said.

Evelyn recounted these supernatural experiences and then went on to say that these things may have caught her attention but her life in Christ was dependent on her daily Bible reading and prayer and her fellowship with other believers.

"Shortly before I got cancer, God told me that I saw everything through egocentric eyes and that I had a lot to learn," Evelyn continued. "Then these unusual things happened, and the love of God and these women encouraged me to more fully submit to the Lordship of Christ. Although I had these experiences, I needed to grow, and all these years, Jesus has been transforming me from the inside out."

In 1974, Evelyn had a stroke. She called Ruby Haff to ask the group to pray because she was paralyzed and couldn't stand up. The group prayed. Pastor John Blewitt, who often ministered at the prayer group, came to the hospital and prayed for her. In six days, she walked out of the hospital completely healed.

Diane Moder is another woman who came to the prayer group following a miraculous healing through the Kathryn Kuhlman ministry.

"I was only ten years old when I committed my life to Christ, and although I was blessed with Christian parents and attended church regularly, I didn't understand how to grow as a Christian, and as I matured, I drifted away from the Christian faith," Diane said.

"During this period of my rebellion, which was back in the sixties, many people were listening to Kathryn Kuhlman, but I didn't like her. Any time I found someone listening to her, I'd say, 'Why don't you turn that crap off!'

"Then, shortly after that, I was diagnosed with kidney disease. A neighbor urged me to go with her to a Kathryn Kuhlman service, and I went and saw people falling down. She told me that the power of God had come upon them. I said to her, 'I'll never do that.'"

"I kept going back, and the fourth week, Miss Kuhlman spoke directly to me and asked me to come up front. As I approached her, I fell down under the power of the Lord and I was healed. What a new dimension! Despite my bad attitude, God healed me, and I wanted to find a place of service.

"I knew about the Wednesday Prayer Group and from what I heard, it seemed likely that I could grow as a Christian and find a place of service there," Diane continued. "I was overwhelmed to see so many people, and the excitement and joy that they were experiencing was incredible to me. I was especially blessed by the music. I felt the presence of the Holy Spirit, and for the first time I raised my hands in praise to the Lord.

"It was a cleansing experience to sing those hymns, and I felt such peace. Someone sang, 'There's a Sweet, Sweet Spirit In This Place' and other praise songs that meant so much to me."

At that time, Diane's son, Mark, was taking guitar lessons and Diane started going with him to the lessons. She watched as the instructor taught him how to play, and when she went home each week, she would practice what she'd observed. Soon she began to learn the songs that the guitarists played at the prayer group.

In 1974, two years after Diane began to attend the Wednesday meetings, Ruby asked her to bring her guitar to the prayer group and help with the song leading. Although

Diane was playing with other guitarists for the first time, she knew the music so well that she was able to follow as one song flowed into another.

"They didn't know that I had taped all their music each week and practiced it at home. That's how I really learned to play the guitar. Getting up front was a challenge, but Jean and the others encouraged me," Diane said.

"The time came when Jean had to go out of town for a week and the others asked me to lead. I was petrified to think of standing in front of all those people and singing when I didn't have a trained voice. The thing that helped me most was remembering what Jean had told me: 'Don't plan what you're going to do. Instead, lean on the Holy Spirit.'

"Through the group, I've learned to depend on the guidance of the Holy Spirit in my life as well as my song leading. The Holy Spirit does a better job than any of us can ever do alone. And I should mention that we do prepare through praying together before each meeting."

Tibb recalled another healing miracle that took place over a period of time through surgery and prayer: "My friend June had a broken hip that didn't heal properly. She came to the prayer group while we were still at the house. She was using a cane and she was in constant pain. It was so bad that her husband filled a pitcher with martinis before he left for work every morning and that would get her through the day," Tibb said.

"I don't know how many times she came, but one day, I felt led to say to June, 'You're to put your cane aside and walk up the stairs and then turn around and walk down.'

"She was terrified at the idea of doing this and said that she didn't think her husband would like her to take such a chance. By faith, I told her that we would catch her if she fell, even though I knew that it was highly unlikely that we could catch her. I just knew she wouldn't fall," Tibb said.

"She walked up those steps, and by the time she started down, she had gained confidence that God was healing her. She faced her fear, and that day she went home without her cane and without her martinis."

"Through these kinds of experiences, God has shown us the truth of His Word and His healing power many times through the prayer group," Tibb concluded. "We pray that His power will continue unabated here for many years to come."

# Chapter 23
## The Tea Party Was Over!

> *"The Spirit of the Lord God is upon me,*
> *Because the Lord has anointed me*
> *To bring good news to the afflicted; He has*
> *sent me to bind up the brokenhearted,*
> *To proclaim liberty to captives*
> *And freedom to prisoners"* (Isaiah 61:1).

TIBB'S HUSBAND, WYNN, COOPERATED IN EVERY way to ease her burden as the Lord increased the size of the prayer group. Each Wednesday morning before he went to work, he set up chairs and brought in sweet rolls. When the numbers increased beyond practicality to sit around a table, the women brought sandwiches, set up trays, and stayed all afternoon.

"It was five years before there were more than you might invite to a tea party," Tibb recalled. "We learned to trust each other, and God honored our commitment to Him, in our personal lives and in our intercessory prayer for others.

"The pattern the Holy Spirit showed us when we were a small group was one that followed the New Testament model. We shared scripture that God had brought alive for us that week. We talked about the ways in which we were applying it in our lives, then we prayed—for each other, for our churches, for our nation and the world," Tibb said.

Sometimes they sang together. Everything they did was very spontaneous. They were responding to the direction of the Holy Spirit as He brought things to their minds and as He spoke to each one who came.

"The group began to grow rapidly in the mid-sixties. People no longer came in pairs. They came by the dozens and then by the hundreds," Tibb said.

"We never advertised and seldom announced speakers. People told me they received Christ while they sat on the stairs that adjoined our living room and even when the only place left for them was in the powder room. The power of God's presence filled these rooms and overflowed onto the porch when people couldn't get inside. Wynn used to call the group our little tea party. By the mid-sixties, the tea party was over."

Among those hundreds who came, many nurses and doctors introduced themselves and she soon counted them among the regulars. She praised God that her background as a nurse reassured them that any physical miracles would be properly substantiated.

"It was part of God's direction for my life that I trained to become a nurse. While I was attending Indiana Normal School for Teachers (Indiana University of Pennsylvania), it came to me that I should go into nursing. There weren't any nurses in our small town of Glen Campbell, near Indiana, Pennsylvania. The town doctor was overwhelmed with patients. Many of them were so poor they couldn't even afford diapers for their babies," Tibb said.

She went home and told her parents that she wanted to go into nurses training. They thought that would be the worst career she could choose, but they didn't stop her.

## The Tea Party Was Over!

"There were times when I, too, thought it was the worst thing I could be doing, but I could always see the need. Imagine a country girl landing in the venereal disease department of a large city hospital. I'd never heard of such things. We had to be so careful about wearing rubber gloves to protect ourselves. I might not like it, but I knew I was to stay," Tibb said.

While she was taking postgraduate work at Columbia University, she was asked to teach pediatric nursing at Bellevue Hospital.

"It was during the Depression and they were rescuing babies out of garbage cans. I learned more than nursing skills. I learned compassion, and apparently they liked my work because they wanted me to stay at Bellevue. They offered more money than I would earn in Pittsburgh, but I was committed to return to this city near my hometown for three years. This was the first time I came here to live after I completed my training."

It was partly a commitment to the needs that had drawn her into nurses' training and partly a commitment to Wynn Gethin, whose family home was not too far from her own.

"Wynn and I met and started to date when I was a college sophomore. He played football, basketball and was head of his fraternity, but he never let that go to his head. He brought me to Pittsburgh to meet his family, and that was very comforting to me as far as the kind of person I thought he was. After Wynn and I were married, we moved fourteen times, from city to city, before we settled down in Pittsburgh and began to experience the work of the Holy Spirit in our lives," Tibb said.

She was brisk in her recital of her background, and her digression from prayer group history to personal history covered only information she considered relevant to the way God prepared the couple for ministry. Without any transition, she returned to telling about the prayer group.

"As the Lord blessed the prayer group ministry with numbers and a multiplying of the healing miracles, there were those women who came who were more flamboyant in style and personality than I was. Sometimes they tried to persuade me to focus more attention on the healing ministry," Tibb said.

"My responsibility has always been to do it God's way. People always called it "Tibb's group" and I tried to discourage that. I had nothing in it. God did it all. He sent the people. They just seemed to flow into my home and later into the church, forming a network of His people. There was a New Testament feeling of Christians melded together from many churches, and as time went on, they came from many nations."

Tibb poured every free moment into studying the Bible, not just academically as her human nature directed, but devotionally so that she could know the heart and mind of God. She recognized that God had a plan for her life long before He led her into the prayer group ministry. She believed that it was no coincidence that early in her career, the director of nursing in a Philadelphia hospital had provided for her training in public speaking. God used her storytelling skills and ability to pepper her talks with humor as a means to bypass the ears and the mind and speak to the heart of people who needed to hear the gospel. She often spoke of God's love, but it was her practice of love that drew people to her and through her to the Lord she served.

"People are so alone," Tibb said. "The hugs do more good than a thousand words." She urged Christians to seek the fullness of the indwelling Holy Spirit and His power for living, and she presented the message of salvation with a compelling urgency to those who didn't know Christ. When the group was large and invited speakers didn't come, she was always prepared to exhort the group to study the Bible—God's Word—in order to live in obedience to the guidebook God had provided for living.

"Some people wanted to put more emphasis on the gifts of the Holy Spirit, and if I had allowed that, various individuals might have been idolized. The church in action never idolizes a person. God would never permit that. He alone is to be worshiped and adored," Tibb said.

"When we are born again, we receive the Holy Spirit, and if we nurture His presence, we will receive the fruit of the Spirit, and these fruits—love, joy, peace, longsuffering, gentleness, goodness, faith, meekness and self-control—demonstrate His character and personality in our lives," she said.

"Paul tells us in his letter to the Galatians that there is no law against these fruits. They will create harmony, and as the Body of Christ produces this fruit, people will become healthy in their spirits. If we focus on this kind of spiritual growth, we will understand what it means to abide in Christ.

"In the Gospel of John, Jesus uses the metaphor of Himself as a vine and His followers as branches. He showed me through the scripture that when I received Jesus as my Savior and Lord—and He is the vine—I became a branch and He grafted me into the vine. I became one with Him. His life flows from the vine into me as a branch, and it's His life in me that produces fruit," Tibb said.

"A comparatively small number of people have been supernaturally healed through the prayer group, but I believe that anyone who comes sincerely looking for a blessing from God will experience the fruits of His Spirit through those who minister in this body of Christ.

"I had to learn to appreciate that the fruits of His Spirit are the true proof that the Holy Spirit is active in the lives of individuals and in the prayer group," she concluded.

God's love, both His gift of love and love that is the fruit of the Holy Spirit, was administered in large doses through the group, and it was a magnet with tremendous power that drew increasing numbers to the house on McCully Street.

Tibb knew that the group was outgrowing the house. Many women who had larger homes offered them, but the Lord was speaking to Tibb about the need to move to a church where more people could be accommodated.

Her pastor had often invited her to move the group into the Mount Lebanon Methodist Church where she was a member. She had hesitated because the prayer group was a nonsectarian fellowship. Many Catholics attended, and she didn't want them to feel uncomfortable.

At the time when the Lord began speaking to her about the urgency of moving to the church, her pastor's wife, Lois Trevor, who often attended the prayer group, sought her out after church one Sunday morning.

"Don't you think it's time to move the prayer group to the church?" Lois asked. "You know the church board is behind the move one hundred percent."

Tibb knew in her heart that God was also one hundred percent behind the move to the church.

# Chapter 24
## Goodbye to McCully Street

> *"Let all things be done properly and in an orderly manner"*
> (1 Corinthians 14:40).

Approximately 150 people attended the last meeting at Tibb's house. Many of them crowded into a local restaurant for lunch with Tibb, Ruby Haff, Ava and Albert Steiner, Jean Yocum, Carol Nomides and others after the meeting. It was a time to celebrate and to talk about what God might do the following week at the church.

Sanner Chapel was reserved for the ten o'clock prayer meeting. It was a large room near the front entrance to the Mount Lebanon United Methodist Church. By 9:30 the church parking lot was filling rapidly. Other cars were parking at the Mount Lebanon U.P. Church across the road. Tibb was stationed at the door of the chapel and her greetings were as warm and homey as if she were standing at the door of her McCully Street home. Tibb was too busy greeting to count, but Clarence Williams estimated that the room would seat 250, and by ten o'clock, it was filled to capacity.

Tibb knew that when her home became overcrowded, some of the regulars had been staying home to make room for newcomers. It seemed that if one person came from a church or a neighborhood in the area, a dozen others might follow. She also knew that each time she spoke at a Pittsburgh area church, new people came to the prayer group.

In 1968, the group gained additional recognition when Tibb served as Prayer Chairman for the Billy Graham Crusade. She helped many churches set up home prayer meetings, and some of these prayer meetings continued after the crusade. The home prayer meeting was gaining new acceptability just as hers was moving into the church.

As the decade drew to a close, news of the work of the Holy Spirit in many Protestant churches was being eclipsed by an outpouring of the Holy Spirit in a prayer group at Duquesne University, that rapidly spread beyond Pittsburgh.

Then there was the expanding work of the Holy Spirit through Russell Bixler's Sunday evening service where he was leading people to be baptized in the Holy Spirit and many people were being healed through his prayer ministry. In the spring of 1970, the second Greater Pittsburgh Charismatic Conference that Russell helped to organize attracted thousands of people.

"Just as we had seen a mighty wind sweep through my home, that same wind of the Spirit seemed to be reaching into every corner of the city," Tibb said. "People from our Wednesday Prayer Group carpooled to the Charismatic Conference, and many testified to the glorious outpouring of the Spirit they witnessed at that conference."

Aside from individual experiences that fueled the excitement at Tibb's meetings throughout the summer of the first year at Sanner Chapel, the group began to pray earnestly that

## Goodbye to McCully Street

God would provide the means for Russell Bixler and other charismatic leaders to develop a Christian television channel. Pat Robertson was the keynote speaker at the Charismatic Conference, and he had challenged his listeners to commit their lives to prayer for the city. He had prayed that God would raise up a Christian television channel that would present the gospel to people who had never heard it before.

Tibb heard of weekly prayer groups at St. Bernard's Roman Catholic Church and in the Greek Orthodox Church, both in Mount Lebanon. After Father George Stockhowe of St. Martin's Episcopal Church in Monroeville and members of his church received gifts of the Spirit, he had erected a huge sign on top of his church on the Parkway East that read "Jesus Is Alive." Members of these churches were praying and reaching out with practical help to those in need.

"It was so thrilling to all of us to have speakers come to our group and tell us of a whole network that was branching out in our city," Tibb said. "And of course, God blessed our move to the church with continued conversions and wonderful experiences of healing."

Within a few months, the chapel was so crowded that Tibb's pastor, Dr. Winston Trevor, suggested that it might be time to move into the main sanctuary of the church. The occasion of a special week of scheduled Bible teaching at the Mount Lebanon United Presbyterian Church next door offered a reason to make an immediate change to the sanctuary. It seemed that renewal meetings in other churches often brought more people to the prayer group.

"The organizers of the 'Come Alive' weekend at the United Presbyterian church suggested that I might like to have their guest Bible teacher speak at the Wednesday meeting," Tibb said.

Tibb listened to cassette tapes they provided and was satisfied that the teaching of Ernest O'Neill, of St. Paul, Minnesota, had a strong Biblical basis, and she liked his emphasis on righteous living.

"Although we never advertised our speakers, the United Presbyterian Church had circulated brochures announcing our meeting as well as their own. More than 450 people filled the sanctuary the day Ernest O'Neill spoke, and what a joyous time of praise and worship we had."

# Chapter 25
## *Going Home with Jesus*

> *When I saw Him, I fell at His feet as like a dead man. And He placed His right hand on me, saying, "Do not be afraid; I am the first and the last"* (Revelation 1:17).

THE LATE DR. CARL NILL RETIRED FROM MEDical practice in 1971. As a physician and head of the medical staff of Allegheny General Hospital in Pittsburgh, he had always felt that doctors are servants of the Lord who use tools and medicine to help bring God's plan for healing to fruition.

His conviction had been confirmed many times, none more dramatic than the night he made an emergency call to see an elderly lady who was very ill. Her daughter said that she couldn't waken her mother. As Dr. Nill was taking the mother's pulse, she opened her eyes and spoke to him.

"Hello, Doctor Nill," the woman said. "Look across the room at the angel on the brightly lit stairway. And Jesus is standing at the top of the stairs. He's wearing a shining white garment. See His arms are extended and He wants me to come up the stairs to enter His heavenly home. I'm going home with Him."

She spoke with an attitude of great joy, and when she finished speaking, she closed her eyes and Dr. Nill felt the sense of her spirit going home to be with the Lord.

In other instances, he saw people get well who, medically speaking, didn't have a chance to survive. He was blessed by these experiences and never doubted that he was sharing glimpses of eternity. God was preparing him to experience a medical miracle of his own.

About a year after his retirement, the doctor returned to the hospital to visit his former colleagues. He teased a heart technician by telling her that she should be working instead of standing around talking to him. She agreed that what he said was true and suggested that she do an electrocardiogram on him while they talked.

"Go right ahead," he said. "But, I surely have no need for it."

It was hard for Dr. Nill to believe the results of the test. It showed that he had a coronary occlusion. It was unusual to have this condition without pain. He decided to check further with a heart catheterization, which verified the tracing. As he and his wife, Dorothy, drove home from the hospital, they prayed, asking God to help them make the right decision about bypass surgery.

Bypass surgery was in its infancy in 1972. In many cases it was totally successful, but whether the results would be long-lasting was yet to be proven. Heart surgeons at Allegheny General Hospital were leading the nation in perfecting this surgical procedure, but Dr. Nill was faced with a decision similar to those he had helped patients to make.

What were the odds for life expectancy if he did nothing? The condition of his heart was such that he could have a heart attack and die at any time. With bypass, if all went well, doctors anticipated that patients could expect at least ten trouble-free years.

The next evening, Dr. Nill and his wife had dinner with good friends—their pastor, Dr. Robert Lamont, and his wife Edna. "Of course, we discussed the decision we had to make," the doctor said.

Early the following morning, Edna Lamont called to invite the Nills to the Wednesday Morning Prayer Group. They accepted the invitation and wondered what benefits they might receive, for they didn't know anything about the group.

Before the meeting began, Edna introduced the couple to Tibb. Then, at the end of the meeting, Tibb invited anyone with a problem of any kind to come forward. Dr. Nill went to the front of the sanctuary and knelt at the altar.

"Tibb placed her hands on my head and began to pray for me," Dr. Nill said. "My body became warm all over—from my toes to my head. I felt so very light that I thought I was floating in air. I cannot explain what happened.

"I rose from a kneeling position and felt strong, so strong. All the fear I had about my heart condition had left me. The Lord touched me that day in a very special way and healed me completely from that heart condition," he said.

He told Tibb what happened. "I just seemed to float back to my pew. It didn't seem like walking at all. I never, ever felt anything like this in my whole life."

The next week, he went to his heart specialist for a check-up. After examining him, the doctor said, "You must have been to another doctor since I recommended surgery?"

"Yes, sir, I have," Dr. Carl said.

"Who treated you?" His doctor asked.

"My Lord and Savior, Jesus Christ," Dr. Nill replied.

The specialist said that there was a whole new blood supply coming into Dr. Nill's heart.

"Well, each time I visited the doctors and nurses over at the hospital, I looked for opportunities to tell them about my faith in Jesus Christ," Dr. Nill said.

"That's exactly what Jesus wants us to do, isn't it? To win souls for Him. To make them realize that He is alive today as much as in Bible times. This should be our top priority, should it not?"

After God healed Dr. Nill, he went to the Wednesday Prayer Meeting whenever possible. Any of his former patients who came to the prayer group saw him anointing people with oil and praying for a miracle of healing.

"I will tell you only one story of the healing ministry God allowed me to share with Him," he said. "The wife of a Methodist minister always came to the prayer group. Her husband never came with her, because he questioned the working of the Holy Spirit and didn't believe in the born-again experience.

"But one day, her husband brought a friend of his to the meeting—another minister who had a serious heart condition and needed help. During the meeting, that minister had a heart attack. Some of the men carried him into the Ladies Parlor, a room in which he could be comfortable. There were seven of us who ministered to that pastor while waiting for the ambulance.

"There I was down on my knees, praying for that man and anointing him with oil, in the name of the Lord Jesus. The Lord's power fell in that place and the color came back into the sick man's face. That minister sat up immediately and said that he felt fine," Dr. Nill said.

"A tall man, named Dan, was standing behind Tibb. She

turned around to him and put her hand on his shoulder and down he went onto the floor under the power of God.

"The preacher who didn't believe in the Holy Spirit turned around to look. Tibb touched him, and down he went under the power. There they were, all those men, lying on the floor in the Ladies Parlor, fallen under the power of the Holy Spirit," Dr. Nill said, laughing at the spectacle that illustrated to him the sense of humor God has.

"It was an important day to remember and, indeed, a real proof once again of the mighty power of our Lord and Savior."

# Chapter 26
## The Mystery of the Turned Chairs

*"And they said, 'Believe in the Lord Jesus, and you shall be saved, you and your household'"* (Acts 16:31).

CLAUDIA AND HER SON WERE IN THE PATIENTS' waiting room at St. Clair Memorial Hospital for a long time. Her husband, Larry, was very ill. One of the members of the prayer group happened to be in the same waiting room and after she heard Claudia's story and her concern for her husband, she invited Claudia to come to the Wednesday meeting for prayer.

The very next week, Claudia and Larry both came and sat in the middle of the sanctuary. That morning when Tibb came down to the front of the church, she told her assistant, Ruby Haff, that they must turn their chairs to face the congregation.

Ruby replied, "That doesn't make sense, Tibb. Why should we do this?"

It was their custom in the sanctuary to sit facing the front of the church when they weren't standing at the podium. Usually, they didn't want to distract anyone's attention from the song leaders.

"I don't know why," Tibb said to Ruby. "I just know

## The House on McCully Street

that's the order the Lord has given me. We're to face the congregation."

Ruby shrugged and turned the chairs and the two women sat down. At ten o'clock, Jean Yocum opened the meeting with a medley of praise songs. Right in the middle of the singing, Tibb noticed that Claudia and Larry were leaving. She had met them at the door and knew this was the first time they'd come and that they had come for prayer. Tibb didn't know what Larry's health problem was, but she knew it was very serious. She quickly got up and followed them out to the narthex.

"Won't you please stay for prayer?" she said to them.

"No, we have to go," Larry said.

"I wasn't about to take no for an answer because now I knew that God must have something special in mind for this couple and He knew they would try to leave. If our chairs had been facing the front as they usually were, they would have slipped out unnoticed," Tibb said.

"Please, let me pray for you before you go," Tibb insisted.

Larry agreed grudgingly. When she finished praying for them, Tibb asked them to promise that they would come back and try the meeting once more. The Lord was speaking to her, telling her that Larry needed to be born again. Once again, Larry gave in to Tibb's repeated exhortation. "All right. We'll come back another time," he said.

Tibb had no idea that Larry was a professional musician and he didn't like guitars. He didn't tell Tibb that he was leaving because he couldn't stand guitar music.

The very next Wednesday morning, the couple returned. That day, a woman who sometimes played for the Methodist church services was accompanying the singing on the organ. She was a professional musician and knew

## The Mystery of the Turned Chairs

how to make the instrument sing. Tibb felt the music was especially worthy of praise that morning with the organ leading and the guitars accompanying the pipe organ.

"Of course, the Lord arranged it all," Tibb said. "He knew how Larry felt about the guitars and didn't want that to stand in the way of his being born again. From that week on, Larry and Claudia came each and every week. He accepted Jesus at the altar of our church and was born again. He lived only two months after that.

"On the day of Larry's funeral, Claudia brought the whole family to the prayer meeting. They said that the change in their father's life before he died made them want what he had. What a celebration we had!" Tibb said.

What if Tibb or Ruby had balked at God's strange direction to turn their chairs around?

"When you walk with the Lord, you recognize His voice," Tibb said. "There's no way we wouldn't follow His leading, even if it doesn't make sense at the time. We needed to turn our chairs to face the congregation so that we could see Larry and Claudia leave. We haven't ever turned our chairs around since then. Never!

"With the Holy Spirit in charge, we pray and follow His directions as we understand them. You know, Jesus tells us in the Bible to ask and that we will receive. And how generous He is to us all, and how much we love Him!"

Tibb emphasized her point by telling another story about the importance of acting immediately when God gives direction.

"Ruby Haff had invited her friend Wilma Haines to come to the prayer group many times, because she felt a special responsibility toward the women in her own church. When Wilma finally came in 1967, Ruby felt like she was pulling her back from the brink of destruction.

"Ruby knew that Wilma had a lot of questions about religion, and during this time of questioning, someone was urging her to read Edgar Cayce's books on reincarnation. She couldn't see the harm in that, because she believed that every religion has something to offer and that all religions have something to help you find your way to God," Tibb said.

Wilma was sitting across the room from Tibb in the Steiner's living room when Tibb began to tell her story for a videotape the group was making. Wilma nodded her agreement, and then she picked up the telling of her own story.

"I was like so many others in the church," Wilma said. "I thought I was a good person. I had attended church all my life and tried very hard to do the right thing. At the prayer group, I learned that there is only one way to please God and that is through the Lord Jesus Christ and that there are a lot of false prophets who want to lead people into false religions.

"I found the truth of God's one way to eternal life through Jesus Christ, and had Ruby not persisted, I might not have ever come to the prayer group. I was reluctant to come despite the fact that I admired Ruby and often noticed her lovely hats. She made all those hats, and I might first notice the hats, but then I couldn't help but notice that she really glowed with the joy of the Lord," Wilma said.

Wilma described the first meeting she attended: "The meeting was surely different than any I ever attended. There was singing—and oh, how beautiful it was! Not the usual church hymns, but songs based on scripture. What a wonderful and easy way it was to learn Bible verses. Tibb always had a scripture to share, and one of her favorites was from

## The Mystery of the Turned Chairs

Paul's letter to the Colossians. This scripture explained the way God wanted Tibb to lead the meetings. Wilma quoted:

*Let the word of Christ richly dwell within you, with all wisdom teaching and admonishing one another with psalms and hymns and spiritual songs, singing with thankfulness in your hearts to God. Whatever you do in word or deed, do all in the name of the Lord Jesus, giving thanks through Him to God the Father* (Colossians 3:16-17).

After the singing, it was Tibb's practice to ask if anyone had a "Thank You," and people would begin to share the stories of how God was answering their prayers.

"I couldn't believe that people were actually telling about being healed. I had never heard anything like this before. It was so exciting," Wilma said.

"Then, when they prayed, it was so beautiful and real. I knew without a doubt that the Lord was listening. I couldn't wait to sit in that blue chair they reserved for people who needed special prayer. When people gathered around to pray, I felt the presence of God in that room.

"Of course, I kept coming back each week. Nothing could have kept me away from those Wednesday morning meetings. There was a different speaker each week. Sometimes, a well-known minister or missionary—perhaps from India or Africa. Other times, the speaker might be a housewife or a businessman. I felt that each one who spoke had a special message from the Lord—a message especially for those who were there. And I listened carefully for what God had to tell me through the speaker," Wilma said.

"That was the beginning of the new birth for me—learning who Jesus really is and how much He loved me and wanted to answer my prayers. I learned about His mercy, patience, loving-kindness and steadfast love for me."

Wilma also told how God brought her through many trials. "Ever since I received Jesus as my personal Savior, He stands with me, despite the fact that I have failed Him many times. He never fails me. He is always faithful and loving. After more than twenty years, I still can't wait to go to those Wednesday morning prayer meetings each week—to see what the Lord will teach us that day. I can't help but close my story by saying that I give all praise and glory to Him."

## Chapter 27
### God Calls a New Senior Pastor

> *I can do all things through Him who strengthens me* (Philippians 4:13).

MEMBERS OF THE PRAYER GROUP WERE ALWAYS thrilled to have the Methodist church pastor, Dr. Winston Trevor, participate in the meeting. When he came, he often stayed after the meeting and prayed with people who came to the altar.

Tibb believed strongly in the fellowship of all believers and in the order God established for the church. When the prayer group met in her home, she felt the support of her pastor and believed that pastors were given to the Body of Christ with special gifts of administration and teaching.

As she relied on the Holy Spirit to guide her, she also committed herself to submission to the pastors God brought into her life as spiritual shepherds. It wasn't good news to her when Dr. Trevor decided to retire, but she looked forward to the man God would call to take his place.

Although Methodist churches function with a great deal of autonomy today, the bishop continues to recommend a new pastoral candidate, subject to the approval of the congregation and the acceptance of the candidate.

Dr. Patrick Albright wasn't looking for another church when Bishop Roy C. Nichol approached him about leaving an Erie, Pennsylvania, church to pastor the Methodist church in Mount Lebanon.

"I was content with my life in Erie," Dr. Albright said when he began to recall the influence Tibb Gethin and her prayer group had on his life.

"I had been in Erie for fourteen years and sent down deep roots. Bishop Nichol urged me to come and talk to the Mount Lebanon board and to stay long enough to attend the prayer meeting that met in the church on Wednesday mornings. He told me that he attended when time permitted and always felt blessed by the experience."

Dr. Albright met with the pastoral relations committee on January 31 and February 1, 1978. He recalls that he doesn't think the committee members could have persuaded him to come, but when he stood in the balcony overlooking the prayer meeting, he felt the thrill of witnessing the vitality of the Holy Spirit. "Had it not been for the prayer group, I might not have accepted the call to Mount Lebanon," he said.

"I always believed in the healing ministry, and Methodists believe that every Christian—every member of the Body of Christ—is given special gifts for ministry. I have always been very ecumenical, and it thrilled me to see the variety of people from all walks of life and many denominations represented in the group. But, of course, my greatest joy was seeing the way Christ was glorified in those meetings."

Dr. Albright believes in intercessory prayer and appreciated that Tibb always prayed for the pastors of the churches represented in the group. He believes that his spiritual life

## God Calls a New Senior Pastor

and that of the church has been greatly enhanced by the group's intercessory prayers.

"I believe the Mount Lebanon Church is a healthy church and the prayer group has a great deal to do with that vigorous life. I never hesitate to send members in crisis to Tibb. The prayer group is a great resource," he concluded.

Tibb's pastor was always aware of the major differences of theology represented in the group and praised God that it functioned seamlessly, without dissension. He appreciated Tibb's emphasis on Jesus' prayer for His disciples in the seventeenth chapter of John's gospel. He reached for his Bible in order to quote the scripture accurately.

"Her teaching was rich with the words of Jesus, and you might see the reflection of her theology in all His words but never more relevant to the prayer group than the passage from what is sometimes called Jesus' high priestly prayer, beginning in verse twenty of chapter seventeen:

> *"I do not ask in behalf of these alone, but for those also who believe in Me through their word; that they may all be one, even as You, Father, are in Me and I in You, that they also may be in Us, so that the world may believe that You sent Me"* (John 17:20-21).

"She was the great synthesizer. I saw it in all her relationships, and I believe this was because she had such a gift of love. Tibb didn't inhibit those with other gifts from ministry in the group, nor did she covet those gifts she didn't believe she had. She often called attention to the teaching of the apostle Paul when he urged new believers to seek the way of love," Dr. Albright said.

For sixteen years, Dr. Albright was Tibb's pastor and saw the power of her faith when she suffered several major illnesses. Soon after he accepted the call to pastor the Mount Lebanon church, he was standing outside her hospital room door at Allegheny General Hospital and overheard the neurologist tell her that she needed to get used to a wheelchair.

"She wasn't ready for that, and there was a great mobilization of prayer interceding for her to be healed. They prayed. She persevered and leaned on that often-quoted scripture, *'I can do all things through Christ which strengtheneth me'* (Philippians 4:13, KJV). She wasn't healed instantly, but within a few months that wheelchair was history."

## Chapter 28
### A Praise and Worship Songbook

> *"This is the word of the* LORD... *'Not by might nor by power, but by My Spirit,' says the* LORD *of hosts"* (Zechariah 4:6b).

ATTENDANCE CONTINUED TO TOP 400 EVERY Wednesday morning through the seventies, and the music was a vital part of the meetings. Jane Shanor, who ran a small publishing business in her home, suggested that she could print a songbook if everyone worked together to compile it.

Song leaders made lists and members submitted the names of their own favorites. Songs were chosen, rights acquired, and then organist Allen Gibbs arranged the music. Many volunteers contributed ideas for the format, and Jean Yocum decided the final placement of each song. She also designed the cover and section dividers.

Entitled, *Praise, Power and Glory; A Devotional Book*, the collection was divided into three sections that included songs that fit each of the three title categories. Ava Steiner wrote a foreword, and the dedication read, "This devotional songbook is dedicated to the glory of God."

## The House on McCully Street

Tibb contributed a short history of the group, and Russell Bixler wrote a testimony titled "What the Prayer Group Means To Us All." An appropriate Bible verse summarized the purpose of each section. Jean was an artist before she became a song leader, and her cover designs were rich with the symbolism of the Holy Spirit.

Tibb was eighty-six years old the day she sat in her living room slowly turning the pages of her copy of the ring-bound book. Although she was growing frail physically, her voice had not lost its vitality, and from time to time, she would spontaneously sing a chorus or tell a story related to the song and the now empty room would again be filled with the glory of the presence of God.

She especially appreciated the scriptures set to music. Many of these were paraphrased from the psalms, and Psalm 100 was a special favorite. "We shall enter His gates with thanksgiving in our hearts...," Tibb sang.

"In memory, I can hear the sound of their many voices singing and see the radiance of their faces as they worshiped the Lord in this room."

Her voice dropped almost to a whisper as she framed the words of some of the titles: "I Love Thee More Than Life," and "Thank You God For Sending Jesus," "Thank You Lord, For Saving My Soul" and "I'm So Glad That Jesus Set Me Free."

"I always felt the power in our praise, for God directed us to praise Him. I once saw angels in the church sanctuary, and I knew that God was pleased with our worship. About a dozen people saw those angels and heard their singing," Tibb said.

"We live by this verse," she said, quoting the verse at the bottom of a page: *"Not by might nor by power, but by My*

*Spirit," says the* LORD *of hosts'"* (Zechariah 4:6). That's from Zechariah the Old Testament prophet, and it became our theme verse. We never neglected teaching from the Old Testament as well as the New. God inspired wonderful prophecies about Jesus in the Old Testament so that His people would recognize Him when He came."

Personal testimonies preceded the pages of songs in each of the three sections of the songbook.

Vadis Robshaw's testimony was one Tibb chose to include in the songbook as an example of healing that showed how God used the prayers of many people when He intended to heal someone.

"God doesn't share His glory," Tibb said. "He wants everyone to know that it is His power alone that accomplishes these great works. He doesn't want anyone to take credit for what He does."

Vadis wrote about the healing of her son's incurable spinal atrophic disease. It was a healing that progressed step by step as Vadis yielded her desire for his healing to submission to God's perfect will for her son's life. She explained in her article in the songbook that, when her son was eighteen years old, doctors told the Robshaws that nothing could be done medically and the young man would soon become physically incapacitated.

Vadis, whose husband Charles was senior pastor of the East Liberty Presbyterian Church, often attended the Wednesday Prayer Group, and the group interceded for her son. In addition, she went from one prayer group to another asking many people to pray for her son to be miraculously healed.

"Among others, we attended a Kathryn Kuhlman Miracle Service, where she prayed for our son who was 150 miles away," Vadis wrote. "After the service, I asked Miss Kuhlman how God could answer a prayer for someone who wasn't in the meeting. 'Don't analyze it,' the evangelist said. 'Simply accept the healing.'"

"We called our son and told him about the intercessory prayer and he confirmed that from the time of the praying, he could feel the improvement. One year later, doctors pronounced him cured. He became a believer in God's healing power, but a few months after the doctor's confirmation of the healing, the disease reappeared in a much more advanced stage. This time he decided he had to go to God directly, through his own study of the Bible, praying privately for God to heal the disease that was sapping his strength. Over the next year he improved greatly, but was not completely healed.

"Then, on a Sunday night, he arrived late at a praise service at Russell Bixler's United Brethren Church in Pittsburgh. He had to stand in the back of the church. A woman who attended Tibb's group and had been healed of liver cancer was sitting in the front row that night facing Russell who sat on a stool leading the service. There was freedom for people to speak out in those meetings in the same way they do at Tibb's, and the woman said, 'God loves somebody here very much. He is filling in holes in the spine the whole way up to the neck.' Russell asked, 'Who is this for?'"

Vadis's son stepped forward, and doctors later confirmed that he was totally healed that night. Ten years later, the young man was a practicing attorney who played tennis and basketball recreationally and was a dedicated Christian who was active in his church. Today, thirty years later, he is head of the Advocacy Department for Mental Health

Agency of his home state, where he is known as a pioneer in this field of service.

"God restored this young man to health in order to fulfill His plans for his life," Tibb said. "God has a plan for each of us if we only ask Him to reveal it."

She continued to turn the pages of the book as she explained that twenty pages of musical selections followed each testimony.

"He's the Savior of my Soul," is the first praise song, and here's "Sing Hallelujah to the Lord," a song that Jean loved to do as a round," Tibb said. "And here's a song that became my theme song, 'This is my Commandment That You Love One Another' and then 'His Banner Over Me Is Love.' Jean always did motions. She'd push the tempo up until the motions overlapped each other. She wouldn't stop until everyone was tongue-tied and laughing." Tibb paused and laughed as she remembered the crowd following Jean's lead.

"Jean could always make us laugh and with this song—'Let's just praise the Lord'—she could get even the most reserved Presbyterians to raise their hands without feeling awkward," Tibb said.

If a hymn didn't fill a page, the editor of the songbook inserted Ruby Haff's poems. Often, Ruby was part of the song-leading team, and it was a special morning when she introduced a new song of praise given to her by the Lord.

"Here's another one to live by," Tibb said. "'Keep me pure, Lord Jesus, keep me pure.'"

She looked up from the book and commented that Jesus sets the standard for purity that we can never attain in this life.

"We cannot achieve purity on our own, but we can yield to God's cleansing power daily to prepare for the work He sets before us," Tibb said.

"This applies to nations as well as individuals, and as a nation, I fear that we are losing the knowledge of what purity is and what it should mean in our lives. Jesus heals our iniquities, but that is no reason to test His mercy and longsuffering toward us."

She paused to comment on another scripture passage set to music.

"This one set the sanctuary rocking," she said, and she quietly sang the words of the chorus, "Walking and Leaping and Praising God." The words retell a Bible story from the book of the Acts in which a lame man is healed through the ministry of the apostles Peter and John.

The song had special meaning to Tibb, for she said Jesus had taken her hand and raised her to her feet on two occasions when doctors believed she would never walk again under her own power.

Her voice trailed off as she riffled through the rest of the Power section to the third section, with songs related to God's glory.

"We never tired of these choruses," Tibb said. "My ears still ring with the memory of these simple tunes inhabited by the Holy Spirit and sung to the glory of the Lord. How fitting that the last song in the book is 'To God Be the Glory.'"

# Chapter 29
## Looking Out for His Flock

*"He [Jesus] said to him a second time, ' Simon, son of John, do you love Me?' He said to Him, 'Yes, Lord; You know that I love You.' He said to him, "Shepherd My sheep"'* (John 21:16).

WHEN JANE SHANOR FIRST CAME TO THE prayer group, she enjoyed the meetings from the safe distance of a back row in the Methodist church sanctuary. After she completed the songbooks, she felt more connected and she began to sit further forward.

"I knew the Lord was nudging me to ask some of the women from my church to come along with me on Wednesday mornings," Jane said.

"Whenever I had the chance, I'd corner one of the women and tell her about the meeting, and as I did this, one by one, more of the ladies were coming with me to the Methodist church."

One morning, in the middle of the meeting, she turned around and saw her pastor Doug Walrath sitting in a back row. She had never mentioned the prayer group to him, and there she sat with a whole row of friends from the church

"I was petrified," Jane recalled. "I loved my pastor and I thought he was doing a great job at our church, but I hadn't had the courage to tell him where I was going on Wednesday mornings. One of the other women must have talked to him about Tibb's prayer meeting."

She knew she had to face him after the meeting or she would spend the rest of her life ducking behind pillars or leaning over a water fountain every time she saw him coming. She didn't know what he would think. Tibb's meeting was different from the usual church service.

"No use putting it off," she thought, wondering if she might be excommunicated. "I took a deep breath and started up that long aisle. He saw me and came forward. I put a smile on my face even though I was quaking inside," she said. "Well, it certainly is wonderful to have you here today, Doug. Why in the world did you come?"

The pastor paused for a moment and then replied, "I'm here because I wanted to see if my sheep were going astray." And then he laughed and hugged Jane.

"If you want to know how he felt about the meeting, I'll tell you that he came every week for many years, unless there was a congregational emergency. And what a wonderful addition he was," Jane said.

Doug was blessed with musical talent. He could sing and accompany himself on the piano. His wife told Tibb that he never sang until he came to the prayer group. Years before, his father had criticized his singing and that squelched his desire to sing. She said the prayer group brought out the music in Doug. He never failed to have some sheet music in his pocket when Tibb asked him to play some special music.

Those who attended the prayer group during the eighties will remember Doug's theme song: "Great Is Thy

## Looking Out for His Flock

Faithfulness." "That song is a hymn of praise, and many of us have turned it into a prayer," Jane said.

The day Doug went up front and knelt at the altar for prayer, he came back and sat down beside Tibb in the first row. He said to her, "Tibb, for the first time in my life, I have found perfect peace in Jesus." Tibb knew that something special happened between God and Doug that day.

"This prayer group has meant life to me, Tibb. This is a place where I can receive as well as give," he said.

"A pastor can be preaching and yet not find what he is seeking for himself until one day the Holy Spirit touches his life in a new way," Tibb said.

Doug and Pastor Bob Caldwell became friends through the group, and when Bob was very ill in the hospital in 1982, he called Doug, who came immediately. The two of them really understood each other.

Ruby often said that many pastors benefited from the unqualified love they received through the people who came to the prayer group. They could lay their burdens at the altar and leave refueled, to minister in the name of the Lord.

## Chapter 30
### Holding the Hand of Jesus

> *"I have loved you with an everlasting love; Therefore I have drawn you with lovingkindness"* (Jeremiah 31:3b).

TIBB MET MAVIS AT A WOMEN'S CLUB MEETING and they became friends. Mavis's lilting English accent immediately identified the country of her origin.

"From the moment I met Tibb, I felt that there was something special about her, even though I didn't quite know what it was," Mavis said when she participated in videotaping a history of the prayer group.

"Something in her eyes and something in her whole appearance made her somewhat different from others. She seemed to shine. Whatever it was, I always wanted to sit near her. I can even remember one Women's Club meeting when I literally sat at her feet."

Mavis's friend Herta also knew Tibb, and she invited Mavis to attend the Wednesday Morning Prayer Group with her if she wanted to find out what was special and different about Tibb. Mavis didn't make excuses for not going to the meeting. Other things were more important to her, and she just didn't go. She did call Herta from Boston in 1986 when her husband, Norman, had an unexpected heart attack.

"I was so relieved when Herta said she was going to the prayer meeting and would ask the group to intercede for my husband." Mavis said. "It was the first time that I thought seriously about that group, and when Norman recovered quickly, I knew that those prayers offered in Pittsburgh were effective."

Still, Mavis put off visiting the prayer group for another three years. It was the week before Christmas in 1989 when she finally accepted Herta's invitation.

"I was overwhelmed by the beauty of the prayer group service. The music was so inspiring that I began to cry. I spoke to Tibb afterward, and she told me that the Holy Spirit was cleansing me, and I knew she was right.

"Norman and I left the next day for a Christmas vacation. All I could think about the whole time I was away was the beauty of that prayer meeting—the people, the music, Carol, Tibb and my friend, Herta, who had finally persuaded me to go."

Mavis began to attend regularly. She realized that there was something missing in her life, a void that needed filling, and she began to yearn for what she learned was a personal relationship with the living God. But she still wasn't quite ready.

"Norman was ill again, and one day, shortly before he was scheduled to go into the hospital for open-heart surgery, I walked over to Tibb at the meeting and I was crying again.

"She said to me, 'This is it; this is it, isn't it?' I went to the altar with her. She had my hand in hers and as she prayed for me, I felt that she took my hand and put it into the hand

*Holding the Hand of Jesus*

of Jesus. When I left the prayer group that day, I felt like my feet weren't touching the sidewalk. I have heard other people talk about that very same feeling" Mavis said.

"I was a different person. I was totally different. I no longer carried the burden of worrying about Norman. I knew that the Lord was going to take care of him. I knew that everything was going to be all right and I felt that I had been really blessed. I was filled with joy and peace and tranquility. I experienced what I had seen in Tibb, and I will be eternally grateful that she was a light upon the path that led to Jesus," Mavis said.

Following her commitment to Christ, Mavis realized a deep longing to join a church. Growing up in England, she had attended the Church of England occasionally but she had never been a member.

"One Wednesday morning, David Watson was the speaker at the prayer group and he recited poetry and played the flute. Of course, I knew right away that he was from England and he was one of the pastors of the Mount Lebanon United Methodist Church where the prayer group meets," Mavis said.

"I talked to him after the meeting and discovered that he was born in the part of England where all my mother's family are from. He was raised in a country town that I knew so well. This seemed confirming direction to me that I should join the Methodist Church," Mavis said.

"Now if I don't get to the prayer group on Wednesday, I feel deprived. And if I don't get to church on Sunday, I miss it desperately. The Lord has made these changes in my life," Mavis said.

Tibb remembered the hot Sunday morning when everyone was swishing their fans in the steamy sanctuary and it seemed likely that many were thinking about getting to the end of the service when they could return to their air conditioned houses. Not Mavis. She came up to Tibb after the service and said that she wished the service had been longer. She wished that it had lasted for at least another hour.

When Tibb told Carol Nomides that Mavis wished the Sunday worship services were longer, she added the comment, "Mavis shines." And in typical Tibb style, she repeated her comment a second time for emphasis, "Mavis shines."

# Chapter 31
## All Things Are Made New

*"Trust in the* LORD *with all your heart
And do not lean on your own understanding.
In all your ways acknowledge Him, and He will
make your paths straight"* (Proverbs 3:5-6).

BARBARA WAS BORN INTO A FAMILY WHO HAD little regard for their faith or for religious training in the home. She was the youngest of three siblings, and their mother made it quite clear to them that she wanted only the eldest daughter.

"Over and over, my mother kept telling my sister Rosemary and me that we should not have been born, that she did not want us, that she could not take care of us," Barbara said.

"Mother used to say to us, 'You are just the scrapings of the barrel.' There is nothing good in either of you.' In her opinion, we couldn't do anything right and therefore we shouldn't even try."

Barbara's mother attempted suicide many times. On one such occasion when Barbara was in the fourth grade, her mother locked a series of doors and then said she was going to drink a bottle of iodine. The child tried repeatedly to get through the doors, pleading and crying out to her mother not to drink the iodine. In desperation, Barbara called the fire department and they broke into the room through a window to find that her mother had already swallowed the iodine. Through their quick action, her mother's life was spared.

"This type of behavior was unfortunately common in our household, and I don't tell you these things to make you feel sorry for Rosemary and me, but so that you can see the great deliverance the Lord provided for me," Barbara said.

As soon as Rosemary and Barbara graduated from high school, their mother told them that the family was going to move from South Jersey to North Jersey. The family had moved twenty times, so this wasn't surprising news until she told the girls they would not be going with them.

"They left us with no special education or training. No money or possessions. We were out on our own," Barbara said.

In November of her last year in high school, Barbara met her future husband. They were engaged at age nineteen and married when they were twenty-one.

"Art had many leadership qualities, but we both brought unhealed hurts into our marriage. We lost our first child but were blessed the following year by the birth of a beautiful baby girl. Eileen was a delightful, loving child. Two years later, baby Tom arrived."

In 1960, Art formed his own consulting company, and his successful business career entailed a great deal of travel. The family moved to Pittsburgh in 1963, and Art began to form a worldwide program for a large corporation. For five years, the family saw him only for a few hours each weekend.

The stress was almost intolerable, and during those five years, Barbara had three major operations, and then she was involved in an auto accident. She went to a psychologist who used hypnosis, and the resulting recollections of her childhood trauma induced thoughts of suicide.

"I felt so alone and abandoned that, mentally, I lost it," Barbara said. "I slashed my wrists."

This was the broken condition Barbara brought to the prayer group. She felt a great sense of guilt for trying to take her life, an act she believed was a mortal sin.

"Even though I wasn't accustomed to Tibb's type of meeting, the love of God drew me. Blanche Breslow and her friend Ginny told me that I needed to be born again," Barbara said.

The two women explained that God had sent His only begotten Son, Jesus, into the world to demonstrate love, and men rejected that love and nailed Him on a cross to die. What seemed a great tragedy was turned to victory when Jesus rose from the dead on the third day and appeared to many of His followers. He told them to wait for the promised gift of the Holy Spirit to be poured out upon them.

"God loves you, Barbara, and He died for you," the women repeated as they explained that being born again meant accepting Jesus, the God-man, as her redeemer and healer.

"They told me that God was extending this gift of His life to me and that I could repent of my sin and He would make me new," Barbara said. "I would be as innocent in His sight as if I were a new baby born that very day. Did I want to be born again?

"With much weeping and repentance, I accepted Jesus as my Savior and Lord. I think I cried for a year and half to think that Jesus, God's Son, loved me. No talent. No special looks. I experienced a verse in the Bible that described me:

'*For my father and my mother have forsaken me, but the* LORD *will take me up*'" (Psalm 27:10).

She believed in the newness that God had given her, and the women in the prayer group demonstrated their love to her in many ways. She needed that human interaction, for she was deeply scarred.

"I often repeated these wonderful words from the Bible: '*Therefore, if anyone is in Christ, he is a new creation; the old has gone, the new has come!* (2 Corinthians 5:17, NIV). I clung to these words for healing. But it took a long time," Barbara said.

Psalm twenty-three was another anchor for her soul: "*The* LORD *is my shepherd; I shall not want. He maketh me to lie down in green pastures: he leadeth me beside the still waters. He restoreth my soul...*" (Psalm 23:1-3, KJV).

"Thank you, Lord, for these promises," Barbara prayed. "I yield to you to complete the healing you have begun in me."

On January 18, 1986, Barbara's son-in-law asked her to pick up her daughter Eileen, who had completed a series of tests related to a back injury. Eileen was a graduate nurse, and during a routine test, she noticed that her white count was unusually high and asked for further testing.

"When I arrived at the hospital, Eileen—who was a very efficient person—was still in bed," Barbara recalled. "It was evident that she'd been crying, and when I tried to comfort her she blurted out the devastating news that she had leukemia. We cried together, but I immediately went to the Lord in prayer. The doctor walked in and said, 'Get your intercessors going, Mom' and that's exactly what I did," Barbara said.

During her drive home from the hospital, Barbara was strangely moved to praise God for the life of her child, and as she did, she felt an overwhelming sense of God's presence in the car.

"The glory of the Lord literally filled the car, and scripture after scripture poured through my mind, and the one that meant the most to me was Proverbs three, verses five and six: *"Trust in the* LORD *with all your heart And do not lean on your own understanding. In all your ways acknowledge Him, and He will make your paths straight"* Barbara quoted.

"I am so grateful for the precious Holy Spirit who led me during the next six and a half years as many people prayed that Eileen would be healed. Each time I went to her home to help her, I would ask the Lord to bring to mind scripture that I might share with her, and I knew with certainty that He was saying to me, 'Just love her.'

"This is what I did. I loved her," Barbara said. "In one of the notes Eileen wrote to me at that time, she told me that she had learned of God's love through me. How thankful I was that out of the pain of my childhood, God had rescued me and taught me to love. It was His love through me that she experienced."

In February of 1990, Barbara noticed that the church was planning an Easter pageant. "The Lord spoke to me and I was prompted to ask if they had a part for an old lady. They had planned to include a scene of Jesus healing the blind Bartimaeus, but since I was available, they decided to use the scene in which Jesus heals the woman with the issue of blood.

"It turned out that the performance was on my sixty-fifth birthday and Eileen, her husband, Jon, and their children came because it was on my birthday," Barbara said. "They were members of the Polish National Catholic Church.

"I believe that, because of the grace of God and the anointing of the Holy Spirit, Eileen's heart was greatly touched. She kept saying, 'I can't believe that was you on stage, Mom.' When the pastor gave the invitation to receive Christ, with tears running down her face, Eileen repeated the sinners' prayer."

From April 1990 until June 15th, Eileen spent a lot of time in the hospital, and Barbara was grateful that she was able to be with her throughout that time.

"On the Wednesday before Eileen went home to be with Jesus, my heart ached as my three grandchildren, Jon, Melissa and Joshua, heard the painful words, 'Mommy isn't coming home anymore,'" Barbara said.

"Eileen was gasping for breath and blood was pouring through the catheter tubing. My heart was breaking, but the Lord recalled those moments in the car six years before, when I had acknowledged that God is worthy to be praised and worshiped no matter what the outcomes are in this temporal life," Barbara said.

"I felt sheltered in the heavenly places, worshipping and praising our King, when the Lord gave me a special message for Eileen: 'My daughter, I brought you into this world whole, and I will bring you into My presence and you will be whole. Release Jon and Melissa and Joshua to me for I will take care of them. My Holy Right Hand rests upon them. I will bring you into My presence, and you will be whole.'

"My sister Patti was watching Eileen's face and saw her respond as I spoke the words God was giving to me for Eileen. We all recognized that, even in death, God cared for her and was directing her."

Even Eileen's burial dress became a special blessing to Barbara and her family.

"God showed my sister Patti a picture of the dress and we simply went out to look for it. It wasn't surprising to us that we found the dress that God had revealed to Patti," Barbara said. "What was surprising was her husband's response to the dress. He told me that Eileen had tried that exact dress on and wanted it, but they couldn't afford to buy it. This was a testimony to us of the minute details of our lives that God is concerned about.

"By God's grace, I was allowed to read the Bible at Eileen's funeral and I was able to minister to people at the funeral home and the gravesite. Eileen was 'absent from the body and present with the Lord,'" Barbara said.

"Do we miss her? Oh yes, we miss her, but when the missing comes, I start thanking God for saving her, for providing an eternal home where there is no more sorrow or tears and where we will be reunited for eternity."

# Chapter 32
## We Are One in the Spirit

> *Therefore many other signs Jesus also performed in the presence of the disciples, which are not written in this book; but these have been written so that you may believe that Jesus is the Christ, the Son of God; and that believing you may have life in His name* (John 20:30-31).

THE UPPER ROOM WHERE JESUS AND HIS DISCIples gathered for their Passover feast may have sounded like the chatter in Ava and Albert Steiner's living room on March 10, 1989.

Tibb had invited people who had attended the prayer group for many years to come and videotape their stories. She told them that God wanted them to prepare for the writing of a book about the miraculous things He had done in their lives. The book would carry the message of God's love beyond its present boundaries.

"I believe God wants to reach a lot of people through our book because it will help people to understand the way He is constantly at work reaching out in ever widening circles," Tibb said.

"A book can reach people who never heard of Jesus and would never set foot in a church or come to a prayer group," Tibb said. "A book can reach people who belong to churches and think they don't have to be 'born again' because they attend church every Sunday.

"I've spoken in so many churches, and it breaks my heart to hear people tell me they are living a good life and that's all they need to be right with God. I ask such a person if their good life is a perfect life—perfect in thought, word and deed. I never met a single person who thought they were perfect and that gives me the opportunity to introduce them to Jesus," she said.

"'Oh, honey, your good works aren't going to gain God's approval. Only the gift of Christ's shed blood on Calvary can do that,' I tell them. 'Jesus has a white robe for you to wear. It's a free gift, and once you put that robe on, God sees only the perfect life of Jesus when He looks at you,'" Tibb said, and those who listened nodded their approval of her words.

Some of those gathered that day at the Steiner's had received that white robe at the prayer group. Others had been introduced to the work of the Holy Spirit in a new way. Some were healed physically, and others received gifts from the Holy Spirit to empower them to reach out to others.

Tibb remarked that many people who came to the prayer group were new converts to the Christian faith, and by the time the President of the Women's Association of her church came, there were new Christians among them who didn't come up to her standards.

"She said to me, 'Look at these women. Some of them don't dress modestly. They smoke. They play cards. You need to get them straightened out.'"

"Now, my friend from the Women's Association was a schoolteacher," Tibb said. "I had to tell her that these were

God's children and He was at work in their lives. It wasn't my business to 'straighten them out.' He's doing the work, and He receives all of us 'warts and all.'

"As those early years unfolded, we were so filled with the Holy Spirit that we were out-praying each other; no pausing between us, just tripping over each other's prayers to agree in intercessory prayer and praise to the Father. It was contagious, and little by little we grew; slowly and solidly we grew, as our confidence in what the Lord wanted to do increased," Tibb said.

Carol Nomides prompted Tibb to tell about Edna Lamont, a minister's wife, who came to the prayer group.

"Edna Lamont came with Mary Friedrich. Mary was a wonderful Spirit-filled Christian who was a member of the First Presbyterian Church in Pittsburgh where Edna's husband Bob was the pastor. Mary brought Edna, and then Edna brought others, including Dr. Carl Nill, who was miraculously healed of a heart condition through prayer at the altar one Wednesday morning," Tibb said.

"Dr. Nill is such a dear man, of the old-fashioned school of doctors. So kind, but formal in a professional way, the way we nurses were taught to be years ago. He came to the altar, and when I prayed, he was healed completely in that instant.

"I've never experienced anything like his healing and the way in which Dr. Nill, who had served the Lord all his life through his medical practice, became a healer in a new way. God used him in remarkable ways as he anointed people with oil at the altar and they were healed.

"I tell you about these people to help you get the idea of the way God is constantly at work through people, leading them one by one in an ever-widening circle of ripples until He has gathered in great multitudes," Tibb concluded.

Someone recalled that Blanche Breslow, a faithful member of the group, had brought a woman named Ginny, who asked for prayer to be healed of terminal cancer.

"She looked like a bag of bones with yellow skin, and she looked so like death that I really didn't want to touch her," Ava Steiner said.

"But we did touch her and let her know that God loved her," Tibb quickly added. "And even though the doctors said she only had a few months to live, we believed that God wanted to heal her."

Pastor John Blewitt prayed for Ginny and she was healed. John was a Presbyterian minister who also attended the Sunday night prayer meetings at Russell Bixler's church and prayed for people there. He and his wife Sarah began to come to the Wednesday Prayer Group while it was still in Tibb's home and continued to help her after the move to the Methodist Church.

"This is the way God brought people to the group, some to help with leadership and so many needing the healing touch of the Lord Jesus Christ," Tibb said.

"Blanche is a dear Christian who brought many people to the prayer group. She and Ginny were used mightily, and both of them led their husbands to the Lord. God used Ginny in the healing ministry here for many years, and then she and her husband accepted a call to full-time Christian service."

Someone reminded Tibb to tell about Bishop Roy Nichol.

"Bishop Nichol would come, and one morning when he was here, Polly Fitzgerald sang, 'There's a Sweet Sweet Spirit In This Place.' I saw the tears streaming down his face, and after the meeting he came over to me and said, 'Surely, Sister Tibb, the Spirit of the Lord is in this place.'"

## We Are One in the Spirit

Many prominent people came to the meetings over the years. Some attended regularly before God called them into ministry. Tibb recalled a wealthy woman who came to the house when seating was so scarce that she sat on the floor near her.

"I watched her face and saw the joy she experienced in this meeting where we were all children of the King no matter what our station in life. Her philanthropy has forwarded the cause of Christ more than anyone will ever know this side of heaven," Tibb said.

Almost everyone remembered the first time Archie Dennis came to the prayer group, where God released him from racial and religious prejudice. God called him from secular work to travel as a singer with the Billy Graham Crusades, and when he retired after visiting eighty countries with the Graham team, he was called to become the pastor of a large multiracial church in Monroeville, a Pittsburgh suburb.

Norman Vincent Peale, the author of many Christian books and founder of the Guideposts ministry, spoke to the group. Michael Harper, a theologian from England, and Dr. Bill Reed, who led the Steiners into a charismatic ministry, were other memorable speakers.

The Cameron Family Singers from Scotland returned many times when they were touring the United States. Kenneth Copeland spoke at the Wednesday Prayer Group before he became well known as a Bible teacher. Bob Woodward from Switzerland, who smuggled Bibles behind the Iron Curtain, told how guards looked at the illegal Bibles in his suitcase and, by the power of God, didn't see them.

Wayne Alderson, who wrote a book about introducing Bible study and prayer into his business life, was a favorite speaker because his heart for Pittsburgh matched the zeal of those who listened to his inspiring words. John Guest, who was an Episcopal rector at the time he spoke to the group, founded the college ministry, Coalition for Christian Outreach, as well as Trinity Seminary in Ambridge, Pennsylvania. Later in his ministry, he organized a crusade ministry that reached into many cities around the world. He continues to have great influence in the Pittsburgh area through his pastorate at Christ Church at Grove Farm in the Sewickley area.

They remembered an eye doctor, Dr. Tom, from India, who inspired them to pray for foreign missions, and a priest named Father Gus, who was healed of blindness and became active in the healing ministry in Pittsburgh. They had a long-standing friendship with Jack Chisholm, who was an associate pastor at First Presbyterian Church in Pittsburgh when he attended the group. God called him to a ministry of prayer and outreach that linked his next pastorate in Sharon, Pennsylvania, with congregations in South Africa. Mary Friedrich reported that Jack started a prayer group in his church that reflected the ministry of Tibb's group.

Individuals called out the names, and the recorded sound of them was like popcorn bursting as the heat penetrated the kernels.

"We've never kept records," Tibb said. "But, we have our memories, and these are what God will call to our mind so that our book will show that God is at work in wonderful ways all around the world."

Carol began to sing "We've a Story to Tell to the Nations," and the others joined her. They sang of darkness turning to dawning as those who know the brightness of the

## We Are One in the Spirit

Holy Spirit residing in their hearts. They sang of the Lord's return to this earth to establish His Kingdom as those who know they will reign with Him. It was a joyous conclusion to a video recording that would become the reference for Tibb's book, *The House on McCully Street*.

# Chapter 33
## Prayer Encompassing the Globe

*"Moses My servant is dead; now therefore arise, cross this Jordan, you and all this people, to the land which I am giving to them..."* (Joshua 1:2a).

TIBB GETHIN DIED IN 1995, SIX YEARS AFTER Carol Nomides's husband, Charlie, videotaped the stories for this book and only a few months after Tibb completed the interviews for the book.

Many people approached Carol after the memorial service for Tibb and asked if Carol would continue the prayer group. Carol believed that God was leading her to continue, but she needed confirmation.

"Tibb always said that the group belonged to God, not to her," Carol said. "God called her to lead the prayer group, and He chose the succession of leaders. Even though I worked alongside Tibb for thirty years, I didn't presume that God would call me to become the new leader." However, a few things had happened to Carol before Tibb died that led her to believe she would receive that call.

Carol remembers that about a year and a half before Tibb died, she had an experience that seemed prophetic of

God's will for her to continue. Carol didn't tell Tibb, but she talked to other leaders in the group and asked them to pray. Tibb was in her mid-eighties and she was becoming frail. They all knew that God might call Tibb home at any time.

Carol recalls the incident: "I was attending a women's Bible conference, and one evening the speaker was finished and started to walk out of the room. Then she turned back and said, 'Is your name Carol?' and I told her it was.

"Then she quoted a few verses from the Bible about Elijah and Elisha and began to personalize them to me. 'Don't you know that your master is leaving and the mantel will pass to you? Don't grab for it but it will be put in your hands.' It made me think seriously about the death of one who was so dear to me and to all the members of the group," Carol said.

After Tibb's death, Carol kept these words in her heart and waited for further confirmation. She did not covet the leadership and she would not "grab for it."

Two weeks after Tibb died, Robert Owens, who was pastor of the South Hills Assembly of God, came to speak to the prayer group. He opened the Bible and read from the first chapter of Joshua: *"Moses My servant is dead; now therefore arise, cross this Jordan, you and all this people, to the land which I am giving to them..."* (Joshua 1:2a).

The speaker turned to Carol and said, "Tibb My servant is dead. Now Carol, come and lead your people into the Promised Land."

"This was the confirmation I was waiting to hear," Carol says. "This confirmed to me that the prayer group would continue, and so it has. Tibb died in 1995, and now it's 2004. For nine years we've continued with a similar number in attendance now as before she died, and miracles still occur."

## Prayer Encompassing the Globe

Carol is humble about the role God has called her to fulfill and praises the work of the dedicated individuals He has called to work with her. Al and Diane Darby were called by God to stand by her, in the same way she supported Tibb. The Overends, the Fahringers and others were called to play major supportive roles.

"I could never be another Tibb. God broke the mold when he made her. There's no way I can replace her, any more than I could become Ruby when she died, and God called me to become Tibb's right hand person. I pray that I can have that same faithfulness that we all saw in Tibb," Carol said.

The style of the meeting has changed very little from the early years in Tibb's home. Every meeting is different, but each bears the imprimatur of The Holy Spirit.

"There is one new development. One of the first things God told me after Tibb died was that I should have a group of intercessors meeting every week before the meeting. Wilma Haines, Anna Mae Hyrb, Anita Jones and Eleanor Toney come early and pray for the presence of God and the freedom of the Holy Spirit to work in our midst."

Carol continues to encourage people to exhaust every medical treatment available, even as they pray and trust God for those things beyond man's ability to heal. She says that Carole Lischer's recent experience of supernatural healing followed a pattern of accepting all the treatments her doctor advised but not accepting his projection that she would live only four to six months no matter what treatment plan he had for her. He might gain a little time for her, but the cancer was so far advanced that no medical treatment could save her life.

Tests, following surgery to remove a large polyp in the

## The House on McCully Street

colon, revealed that malignant cells in her lower intestine had spread to her liver, lungs, lymph system and pancreas. Carole Lischer knew she had been under a lot of stress, but who doesn't deal with stress?

"I asked the usual question, 'Why me, Lord?' I thought I was the least likely candidate. I followed the health rules and was so healthy that I'd never even had to take an aspirin for a headache, not to mention trusting God, serving in my church and living as good a life as I knew how, based on what I read in the Bible," Carole said.

She believed that God had the power to supernaturally heal her, but would He choose to do so? What lay ahead in the months of chemotherapy treatments, blood tests and CT scans?

She remembers that when she first began to pray, she didn't plead for healing. She simply said, "Lord, I don't know what You want to do with my life, but I surrender my life totally to You. I'm Yours, whether I live or whether I die. Do with me whatever is pleasing to You; just let me spend the time I have getting to know You better."

"Immediately, I felt enveloped in peace such as I've never experienced before. It was like God put my husband, my daughter and me in a little bubble of security. We had absolute confidence and trust in God," Carole said.

"I never heard voices or anything dramatic like that, but I knew in my spirit that God was saying to me, 'I receive you. It's going to be all right. I'm working in you so that I can then work *through* you,'" Carole quotes the words just as she heard the inner voice speaking to her.

"I thought about this and decided that God might be going to teach me principles that I could apply to my life and then pass on to others. Even though each individual is unique and God deals with each one differently, there are principles in the Bible that apply to everyone."

*She believes the first principle of prayer for healing is embodied in the word "surrender."*

"Surrender meant to me that I needed to set aside my plans and wait attentively on the Lord to reveal His purpose and plan for me through my Bible study. Pursuing His presence became my top priority," Carole said.

In answer to her question, "What do you want me to do?" she believes God told her to focus on Him totally. She resigned from all the volunteer work she was doing and set aside the major part of her day to read the Bible and other Christian books. She made notes of things that seemed to apply to her situation while praying that God would draw her closer to His heart.

*She had identified her second principle of prayer for healing: focus on the Lord Jesus Christ.*

To focus on Christ meant to her that she stopped watching television programs that portrayed violence and anything alien to the Word of God. She watched the Christian network, Cornerstone TeleVision, with its emphasis on Bible teaching, and while she worked around the house, she listened to beautiful taped songs of praise, singing along with the music. Aside from her responsibilities to her family, she spent her time searching the scriptures for the many references to the miracles that Christ performed.

"As quickly as I could, I applied the teachings of the Bible to my life. I learned that there was plenty of reference to the disciples of Christ meeting together to pray. That's when I knew I had to return to the Wednesday Prayer Group. I had attended in the past, but I had slipped out of the habit. I knew I needed to return to regular prayer with other believers," Carole said.

*"I believe God led me to associate with as many praying people as possible who would support my faith and surround me with love. That was the third prayer principle."*

Her friends, Winnie and Bob Evans, invited her to go with them as she returned to the Wednesday Morning Prayer Group where many were supporting her with prayers for complete healing. "I experienced the love of the Lord at each meeting," Carole said. "I am in awe of the faithfulness of those who pray for me continually and I'm grateful beyond words."

From the beginning, Carole told her oncologist that many people were praying that God would heal her despite the gloomy medical report. As the weeks passed and her tests showed continual improvement, her doctor was amazed and said, "Whatever your friends are doing, tell them to keep it up."

In January 2002, when the doctor declared that Carole Lischer's blood work and other tests showed that she was disease free, the Wednesday Prayer Group, her neighbors, church friends and others rejoiced with her that God had answered their prayers. She has been cancer free for two years at this writing.

Carol Nomides says that one of the most thrilling aspects of her long-term involvement with the Wednesday Prayer Group is witnessing God at work to heal the sick, save the lost and interact with networks of people who have gone out from the group to minister to the needy across the community, the city of Pittsburgh and around the world.

"Their stories would fill a dozen books, and with our finite minds, I don't believe we could possibly track God's work through the prayer group," Carol Nomides says.

She sees the multiplication principle that fueled the growth of the prayer group continuing to flourish through the lives of those who have attended the group and through the lives of their children and others who have heard the message of Christ through them.

"Diane Moder's son Mark, who joined his mother in leading music for the prayer group during the summer he was sixteen, has a special place in my heart because he is the pastor of the church I attend. God has gifted Mark with the love of Christ he witnessed in the prayer group," Carol says.

She introduced Ernie Frederick to those who attended a recent meeting. His late wife, Lita, had come to the group with her friend Jackie Vereen and then suggested that Ernie take some time off from his job with Youth Guidance, Inc. (now renamed Family Ministries, Inc.) to see what was going on at the Mount Lebanon prayer group.

"I came, and I was startled when I saw the number of people at a prayer group. And I was a little scared at the faith and power of the prayers I saw and heard here," Ernie said. "It had a tremendous impact on my life, for it was through the group that I saw I needed to grow in my prayer life."

He began to study God's principles of prayer spelled out in the Bible. He memorized these principles over a long period of years, and in 1992, he organized a program called "Forty Days of Prayer Walking" prior to the Greater Pittsburgh March for Jesus. This was the first of many prayer-walking events he organized that include his teamwork with "Youth with a Mission" to involve churches in workshops where Christians learn how to set up "Open Air Places of Prayer." If you come to Pittsburgh for the New Year's Eve "First Night," The Pittsburgh Marathons, The

Three Rivers Arts Festival, or other local Community Festivals, you may find these quiet stations for prayer in the midst of the hustle and bustle of the event.

The Wednesday Prayer Group supports Ernie's various Pittsburgh prayer outreach ministries and his current partnership with the Christian churches of Cameroon, Africa, where he has volunteered to teach the Bakossi people to read and write their mother tongue so that they can read the gospel in their own language. During his annual month-long spring teaching trips, he presents workshops on "Scripture in Use and Prayer." Baptists, Roman Catholics, Lutherans, Full Gospel and Presbyterian churches are working with Wycliffe Bible Translators in this translation and literacy work.

"Since I've retired from my official job with Family Ministries, God calls me to straddle the continents of the world," Ernie said. "I've thrown out the word *retirement*. I call it "re-fire-ment." This is a way of life Tibb Gethin understood well for she had a vision of the one-world church of Jesus Christ."

That same Wednesday morning, Carol Nomides invited Tom and Luanne Aitken to talk to the group about their work in Southeast Asia. She prefaced her introduction with the background of their experience with the Wednesday Prayer Group.

"Many years ago, Tom and Luanne attended the prayer group, and we prayed for the restoration of Luanne's sight and she was healed. Later, they came for a twelve-year period, until God called them to the mission field. The Aitkens founded the faith-based Bridges International, Inc., a mission group that has representatives in a number of countries. The purpose of Bridges International, Inc. is to strengthen and encourage existing Christian ministry work worldwide. They provide pastoral ministry to native pastors and missionaries as well as aid for the poor and refugees," Carol told the group.

Tom showed a film in which two refugees from the Moluccu Islands of Indonesia were leading the singing in a prayer group in Bali.

"These young men and others call us 'Mom and Dad,'" Tom said. "They know what it is to flee for their lives. We have visited underground churches in communist countries where soldiers come in and arrest the pastors and scatter the people. When we met with these Christians, they were continually looking over their shoulders, watching the door. Jesus died for these refugees, and He stoops down to raise them up from the dust, just as He died for us and stoops down to raise us up from the dust of sin and death."

Tom opened his Bible and read verses from Psalm 113 to the group:

*The Lord is exalted over all the nations; his glory is above the heavens. Who is like the Lord our God, the One who sits enthroned on high, who stoops down to look on the heavens and the earth? He raises the poor from the dust and lifts the needy from the ash heap* (Psalm 113:4-7, NIV).

Tom looked up from the Bible and commented that God in all His glory is moved to act on behalf of the needy. "We've seen Him do miracles here on the Earth. Tibb and Carol have always pointed out the greatness of God is coupled with compassion," Tom continued. He paused and looked from one person to another across the room.

"When we walk the streets of these foreign lands, we do not go alone. You are with us through your prayers, and we feel your presence with us," Tom said. "We go out from the Wednesday Prayer Group as your representatives, knowing that we serve a risen Savior. He has called us to be your representatives as we take the message out to the people of the world.

"The work of the Wednesday Prayer Group is like that of Aaron and Hur when they physically held up the arms of Moses as he stood on the hilltop overlooking the valley where the Israelites were doing battle for the land God had promised to them." (Tom was referring to the words of Exodus 17:12, NIV).

"The Bible tells us that when Moses held his hands up, the Israelites prevailed, and when his arms became heavy and he lowered his hands, their enemies prevailed, so Aaron and Hur supported the arms of Moses until the battle was won," Tom said.

"The prayer group shares that ministry of upholding Christians in all walks of life, but especially pastors and missionaries. We were strengthened by the time we spent coming to the group every week, until we were called to go out and support other pastors around the world. In the many dangerous and difficult places where we go, we continue to experience that support from this group," Tom said.

"Remember the prophetic promise of the Father in Psalm 2: *'Ask of Me, and I will surely give the nations as Your inheritance, And the very ends of the earth as Your possession'* (Psalm 2:8). We see this promise fulfilled as the prayer group faithfully prays," Tom concluded.

If Tibb Gethin were attending the Wednesday Prayer Group today, she surely would say, "These people shine." She might quote the prophet Daniel's words:

*Those who have insight will shine brightly like the brightness of the expanse of heaven, and those who lead the many to righteousness, like the stars forever and ever* (Daniel 12:3).

The Wednesday Prayer Group that God called Tibb Gethin to start in her small house on McCully Street has played a role in the lives of thousands of people for almost fifty years. Those who come under the influence of the prayer group continue to go out to live transformed lives and to share the gospel of Jesus Christ with their contemporaries. Her influence continues to be a blessing to those in her home community, in the Greater Pittsburgh Area, in the nation and in the world-at-large.

The light of the Lord Jesus Christ shone through the ministry of Tibb Gethin and continues to shine through those whose lives she touched. She was a shining star in God's firmament, engaged in the work of lighting thousands of other "stars" as they joined her in the service of Jesus Christ. God alone knows the extent of "shining" He generated through Tibb Gethin's single-minded obedience to His direction.

CPSIA information can be obtained at www.ICGtesting.com
Printed in the USA
LVOW06s1954191114

414536LV00001B/166/A